ZION CHURCH OF THE CITY OF BALTIMORE · 1755 ·

ZION

IN BALTIMORE

1755 ⟫⟪ 1955

ZION CHURCH · 1955

Erected in 1807

ZION

IN BALTIMORE

1755 * 1955

THE BICENTENNIAL HISTORY

OF THE EARLIEST GERMAN-AMERICAN CHURCH

IN BALTIMORE, MARYLAND

by

KLAUS G. WUST

Published by

ZION CHURCH OF THE CITY OF BALTIMORE

BALTIMORE, MARYLAND, U.S.A.

1955

Copyright 1955 by ZION CHURCH OF THE CITY OF BALTIMORE
Press of Schneidereith & Sons, Baltimore, Maryland, U.S.A.

Dedication

THIS BOOK *is gratefully dedicated to the pastors and parishioners of Zion Church; to the men and women who two centuries ago courageously founded her in faith; to those who for two centuries loyally nurtured her in love; and to those who, in centuries to come, will steadfastly continue her message of hope in the living Christ.*

DIESES BUCH *ist den Pastoren und Gemeindemitgliedern der Zionskirche in Dankbarkeit gewidmet; den tapferen Maennern und Frauen, die vor 200 Jahren die Gemeinde gegruendet haben im Glauben; denen, die durch 200 Jahre die Gemeinde treu gepflegt haben in Liebe; und den kommenden Geschlechtern, die festhalten an der Botschaft des lebendigen Christus, unserer Hoffnung.*

Our Church

ZION CHURCH is two centuries old. Situated in the heart of Baltimore, it is a landmark known to every Baltimorean. For two centuries Zion Church has held its place as the oldest and, for most of this time, also the only Lutheran congregation of German language and tradition. From the early days in 1755, when the little flock of Lutheran immigrants assembled in private homes for worship, down to the present time, services have been held in the tongue of the immigrants from the Fatherland. Founded as the "High-German Evangelical Lutheran Congregation of Baltimore Town," it has ever since been known as the "German Church." But "Zion Church" as it has been called since 1785 is a truly American Church.

Older than the American Republic, older than the State of Maryland, it has witnessed the entire epic of the American nation. Thus, this history of Zion Church is a chapter of the history of Baltimore, of Maryland, and of the American nation. Too often historic research is associated with things of the past alone. This volume, sponsored by the congregation of Zion Church itself, required a research different from the study of extinct cultures or isolated events of history that have long since been forgotten. Zion Church is old, but not aged. The forces which made it grow and decline, rise again, and continue with undiminished strength to this very day, are ever present among the congregation. As in the days of its founding, when a humble harness-maker and a prominent physician took the initiative to establish a fold for their Lutheran countrymen, Zion Church has remained the church of the people. In making a day's calls, the pastor may come to homes where the butler will take his hat and usher him into a stately room, and soon afterwards enter a grim cold-water flat, where he must leave money for rent and for the children or food for the next meal.

Zion is not only a church for the people, but also a church by the people; it is a congregation in which, time and again, laymen have risen to conspicuous leadership. It is a church of struggle for faith. The leaves of this history will relate many an instance where discord and dissension reigned among the members. As deplorable as some of these events will seem to a posterity of men and women who strive for unity and concord, the frequent struggles have made Zion Church the strong bulwark of faith which it now is in the city of Baltimore. Being the mother church of the Maryland Synod of the United Lutheran Church, Zion has exerted a strong influence on Lutheranism in the state and the country.

The aim of this history has been to present an accurate account of two hundred years for the members and friends of Zion Church. It is the story of its people, the pastors and the members who made and lived its history within our community and our nation. The significance of this church in our city and state as a vessel of spiritual and moral strength has often been attested. Probably no finer testimony has ever been given than in the address delivered in Zion Church on October 21, 1951 by Governor Theodore R. McKeldin of Maryland:

"Here is a church that is older than the nation itself. It can truly be said that a great city grew up around it. The location of this fine edifice in the very shadow of our great public buildings is perhaps symbolic. Adjacent to the headquarters where the alarms of fire and sometimes of worldly disaster sound through the day and the night, it is as though a great voice were saying 'There is the symbol of worldly turmoil and uncertainty; here is the sign of calm and the assurance of eternity.'

"Over on the other corner is City Hall, seat of man's municipal government. There laws are made nearly every week. There laws are found unsatisfactory and repealed. Here in the shadow of City Hall's dome, no new laws are made and the old laws never can be repealed. They were written for all ages of man.

"This old church has seen the United States in all its wars. It has seen crisis follow crisis, and has seen each crisis pass. The spirit of Zion Church, living through one generation into another, knows how groundless are the fears of many today that only disaster can come from the present madness which appears to grip the world. Thus, Zion Church, itself a bulwark of our strength as a people, as a City, as a State, and as a Nation, also is a symbol and even a testimony of hope."

HERMANN STEINGASS
President of the Church Council

February 1955

Appreciation

THE CHURCH COUNCIL OF ZION CHURCH records its deep appreciation to Mr. Klaus G. Wust for having undertaken this complete, comprehensive and conscientious chronicle; to Professor Abdel R. Wentz of The Lutheran Theological Seminary, Gettysburg, and Professor Katherine Kressman Taylor of Gettysburg College for their help in the final preparation of the text; to Dr. Johannes Wicht of Hyattsville and Wiesbaden for contributing the drawings which greatly enhance the value of our publication. A last word of thanks is due to Professor Dieter Cunz of the University of Maryland for his advice and assistance during the years when this project was conceived, carried out and completed.

Table of Contents

O *give thanks unto the Lord, for He is good:
for His mercy endureth for ever.*

CHAPTER ONE

Laying the Foundation

"A FEW YEARS after the town of Baltimore was laid out, several German families betook themselves thither to live, of which Vitus Hartweg, harness-maker, was the very first. They were mostly of our Lutheran confession. They were too few to establish a congregation, although after some time more, both Lutherans and Reformed, gathered there. Therefore, the members of both confessions had for their edification to put up with sermons of itinerant preachers, often of bad reputation and conduct." With this statement begins the first account of the religious life among the Germans in Baltimore in the "Kirchen-Archiv, or Curious Description and Account of the Beginnings of the German Lutheran Congregation in Baltimore Town, in Baltimore County, in Maryland, and its progress."

Some of these first Germans in Baltimore had come straight from the Old Country, others from the German settlements of Pennsylvania, especially from nearby York County. For the most part they were pious people. Those who had lived in Pennsylvania before they settled in and around Baltimore, which was laid out as a town in 1729, were no longer untried immigrants. They had already had some taste of American life and were aware that they would have to take their ecclesiastical affairs into their own hands. There was no church organization which would look after them and provide a pastor and initial funds as was the case later, after the Lutheran Church in Pennsylvania became well organized. Their only hope for attracting a preacher and proceeding to form a congregation lay with themselves.

As in all the other settlements of Germans in colonial days, devotional life was, at first, centered in the homes. Many had brought their Bibles and their hymn-books with them from Germany, and generally a few devotional books. To this day some of these volumes are preserved in the library of Zion Church. We find among them Martin Luther's Catechism and Johann Arndt's *True Christianity,* all of them well-thumbed. They were read in the family circles of the first Lutherans, and, as had always been the custom in German families, the father would lead the prayers. Soon several families began to gather together for devotions, and their meetings became regular. The humble dwellings of the townfolks were the first places of worship.

Legally, the position of the Lutherans and Reformed in Baltimore was extremely difficult. Maryland was still a colony of the British crown and the Church of England alone was established by law and supported from the public treasury. By a law which had been in force since 1692 an annual tax of forty pounds on each taxable person was levied for the purpose of maintaining Anglican churches and the Anglican clergy. There was no restriction on founding any other religious body in the Maryland colony, but the tax for support of the Anglican Church had to be paid, regardless of whether a person belonged to another denomination and contributed to his own church. Fortunately the British authorities did not always enforce this law, particularly when a congregation which followed its own persuasion was well organized.

The Lutherans in Baltimore thus belonged legally to the Anglican St. Paul's parish. About 1750 they began to hold their worship in St. Paul's Church together with their Reformed brethren. "These devotional meetings, in commendable harmony, were for some years held in the English church, until baleful envy, or I do not know what, caused the interdiction of further use of the building, whereupon there had to be considered means by which worship could be continued," recalled the chronicler some twenty years later. The English rector, the Rev. Thomas Chase, seems to have been favorable toward the Germans at the beginning as was the case in other towns in Maryland. As for his sudden change of mind, we might find the explanation in a growing distrust of the strange itinerants who served the German Protestants at their Sunday meetings, rather than blame it on "baleful envy." If we have a closer look at some of the individuals who imposed themselves on the Lutheran groups in Maryland in those years, we can readily understand the dissatisfaction of the Anglicans with the use of their venerable church by the Germans.

From the records of the only other Lutheran congregation in Maryland at that time, the Monocacy Church, we can gather what the first account of the Lutherans in Baltimore meant by "itinerant preachers of bad reputation and conduct." There was a vagabond parson by the name of Valentine Kraft, who after having been dismissed for misconduct by the Church authorities in Germany, tried his fortune in America. He wandered about from place to place in Pennsylvania, where, among other things, he served a prison term for violation of the civil law. After his release he turned toward Maryland, where he visited the scattered Lutherans from 1749 until 1752. In the early summer of 1751 the jobless German schoolteacher Streiter appeared in Maryland and imposed himself on the needy congregations. He had never received an ordination from any church. In Frederick he caused a disruption of the Lutheran congregation and aroused the opposition of the Anglican Church. His immoral living was repeatedly recorded. Such unscrupulous vagabonds contributed no little to the plight of the good people of Baltimore who were thus betrayed in their efforts to provide divine services for themselves and their children.

In the spring of 1753 the Lutherans of Baltimore could have secured an excellent minister, but their little flock of eleven souls, most of them having not much more means than were necessary for a modest living, could not raise the amount of money required to "buy" a gifted young theologian who was put up for sale in Baltimore. The Rev. Samuel Schwerdfeger, a native of Bavaria, when twenty-four years of age, had fallen into the hands of emigrant runners, who shipped him as a redemptioner to Annapolis. The Lutherans of York, Pennsylvania, finally raised the money to pay for his passage and virtually "bought" their pastor. They had no reason to regret their bargain as the Rev. Schwerdfeger turned out to be a fine minister, who later served the church of Frederick with much distinction.

In the first years of the fifties many Germans came to Baltimore. They seem to have recognized the advantages of the small town as a place of commerce and trade. Annapolis then was still the dominant seaport of Maryland. It had been incorporated one hundred years earlier, and the English authorities did not attribute much importance to Baltimore. Still, in 1754

Governor Horatio Sharpe wrote to Lord Baltimore: "I have taken an Opportunity since my arrival of visiting Baltimore, which indeed has the appearance of the most increasing Town in the Province, tho it scarcely answered the Opinion I had conceived of it: hardly as yet rivaling Annapolis in number of Buildings or Inhabitants; its Situation as to Pleasantness, Air and Prospect is inferior to that of Annapolis, but if one considers it with respect to Trade, the extensive Country beyond it leaves no room for comparison; were a few Gentlemen of fortune to settle there and encourage the Trade it might soon become a flourishing place, but while few besides the Germans (who are in general Masters of small Fortunes) build and inhabit there, I apprehend it cannot make any considerable Figure."

The little flock of Lutherans and Reformed had every reason to be discouraged: their good faith having been abused in an abominable manner by vagabonds, and themselves being deprived of the privilege of worshipping in the Anglican Church, they again had to assemble in private homes to sing their hymns together and join their voices in common prayer. But they desired more than this. They were longing for the word preached in their mother tongue and for the sacrament of Holy Communion. There were infants to be baptized, and among the younger people there were couples who wanted to be married. The time had come when either they had to find a pastor who would minister to them with some regularity or they would have to join the only church in their town, the Anglican Parish, which meant giving up the faith of their fathers, for which they had been willing to make sacrifices in the past.

There were many Lutheran congregations in the country pleading for the services of a pastor. Only a few of them in Pennsylvania had consolidated sufficiently to carry on a regular existence as Lutheran churches. Untiring ministers were constantly roaming four or five counties in order to keep the congregations together until ministers should come from the Mother Church in Germany to take over these charges. In nearby Pennsylvania, a young clergyman who had just arrived from Germany in 1752, and who, since March, 1753, had been the regular pastor of the Conewago Lutheran Church, tried to reach as many scattered Lutherans as possible. His circuit apart from his own resident charge included all the far-flung Lutherans in the Pennsylvania counties of York, Cumberland, Adams, and Franklin. Although distance was no hindrance for young Pastor J. George Bager (or Baugher as he was later called), he saw no way to include Baltimore in his circuit.

An unexpected event, however, forced the Rev. Bager to abandon some of his visits to outlying congregations in the Western parts. The war with the French had broken out, and French and Indian raiders endangered the roads of Pennsylvania. 1755 was the year of Braddock's defeat by the French and the Indians. Pastor Bager at once turned his efforts toward the neglected field where he could still be of service. He remembered the pleas of the Lutherans in Baltimore and did not hesitate long to offer his services to them, at least temporarily, although it meant that he must ride sixty miles on horseback in order to reach them.

The faithful Lutherans of Baltimore could not offer much to their first pastor. "The first regularly officiating pastor was the Rev. John George Bager, who for three consecutive years came down from Pennsylvania six times a year, administering the spiritual functions in preaching and sacraments, and enjoying from this not more than five pounds per year. This was next to nothing indeed, as a reward for the painstaking of a spiritual guide," wrote the chronicler of the Church under whose anonymity we can suspect the physician, Charles·Frederick Wiesenthal, who came to Baltimore in 1755, the same year Pastor Bager officiated for the first time.

Although we have seen that the Lutherans of Baltimore joined together for worship and devotion prior to this year, 1755 is set down as the actual beginning of the congregation as a distinct organization. Up to this time, Lutherans and Reformed had banded together. In 1755 all those among the Germans whose faith was founded on the "Augsburg Confession" formed the "Evangelical-Lutheran Congregation at Baltimore Town."

The coming of Pastor Bager filled the people with joy and gratitude. The years of uncertainty seemed to be over. Now they had a spiritual guide—the rest of the tasks they would cheerfully do themselves. Moritz Wörschler, a German teacher, and Dr. Charles F. Wiesenthal were instrumental in organizing the congregation. There were many details to be settled. "Everything was well attended to, but mostly by men who were eagerly engaged in the cause, Wörschler, as schoolmaster, attending to most of the

affairs. He collected the little money subscribed for the preacher."
Thus the annalist recorded, with a modesty that lets us again sur-
mise that the actual writer of the church chronicle was Wiesenthal,
whose eminent part in the forming of the congregation is evident
from numerous other sources.

Plans for the erection of a Lutheran church were discussed. But
the congregation was too weak as yet to take such a financial burden
upon itself. Since the Reformed had also organized at about the
same time, the Lutherans proposed a union meeting to consider the
building of a common church, as had been done in numerous other
American towns. The harmony prevailing up to this time between
the two German groups inspired the Lutherans with great hopes
that united with their Reformed brethren, they might accomplish
what seemed impossible to be done by either group alone.

At this meeting, which took place about one year after Pastor
Bager had commenced to serve them, after some discussion, both
congregations resolved:

1. That a tract of land be bought in common for a church and
   a graveyard.
2. That a common church be built.
3. That as long as neither of the congregations had a resident
   minister, any visiting minister of either confession should be
   welcome to use the church. Should both congregations engage
   resident pastors to preach every Sunday, morning and afternoon service should be conducted alternately.
4. That in the case both congregations should increase to such
   an extent that the church became too small, church and graveyard should be sold to one of them, the one paying back to
   the other congregation the equivalent of its contribution.

This plan was enthusiastically received by both congregations.
Alexander Lawson, a well-known merchant, had a lot for sale on a
hill near the old bridge, which seemed most suitable for the purpose
of erecting a church. A delegation consisting of Moritz Wörschler
and Charles F. Wiesenthal for the Lutherans, Valentine Loerch and
Conrad Schmidt for the Reformed congregation, was selected to
arrange the purchase. Conrad Schmidt, a stonemason, who had
formerly worked for Lawson, took it upon himself to bring the
matter before the owner of the lot and to predispose him to make

favorable terms. Obstacles soon arose when Schmidt reported that Lawson was unwilling to sell to the Lutherans. The Lutherans voiced their surprise: "We could not see why Mr. Lawson should not take Lutheran money just as well as that of the Reformed; as the land was in reality in the market." When Conrad Schmidt, however, added that he was convinced the proposed union would cause conflict, the Lutherans began "to fear a Jesuit trick."

Soon the matter was cleared up: "It happened that the Reformed preacher Lachey asked a certain Richard Croxal for another lot on the hill to build a German church there. The latter was so generous as to give one at once without pay for that purpose. Now the murder was out, for the Reformed gentlemen all of a sudden declared openly that this land was given to them alone, they having asked for it, and that they did not care for the union any longer. Thus we poor, credulous Lutherans had, as in other cases, to go away with a flea in the ear."

From the manuscript record we know that the Lutherans did not accept this decision without protest. One of them, Jacob Rach, took his yardstick and walked to the iron foundry where Mr. Croxal lived, two miles from town. We do not know whether Rach's yardstick had anything to do with Mr. Croxal's answer that "he had given the land to the German inhabitants in general, having supposed that they were all of one religion." Jacob Rach, however, was not content with that. He asked Mr. Croxal, a Catholic, whether or not he was aware "that the Reformed, in the Heidelberg catechism, called the Catholics idolators, which also meant him, Croxal. The intention of Rach was doubtless to prejudice Croxal against the Reformed"—the manuscript states with gentle reproach. Mr. Croxal replied that no expressions of the Heidelberg Catechism seemed to be directed against him personally— "which clearly proves that not all Catholics are as bad as they are often depicted." When Rach informed his brethren of his visit to Croxal, they felt "we could not in all things approve of the zeal of our brother. Howbeit we have to overlook these hot expressions, caused by the intrigues and the double-dealing conduct of the Reformed."

Mr. Croxal kept his word and later really paid the Lutherans seven pounds, the value of half the lot. The whole scheme of a union, however, had come to an end.

Now the Lutherans decided to test their own strength although they were much smaller in numbers than the Reformed, who had completed their humble house of worship in 1758. The members of the Lutheran congregation met and deputed Moritz Wörschler, Charles F. Wiesenthal, William Hackel, Caspar Grassmuck and Michael Tiefenbach to enter into new negotiations with Mr. Lawson for the same property which had been proposed as a building site when the plan of amalgamation was in its first stages. The old manuscript recounts the progress of the delegation thusly: "It was necessary, however, to ask this man first whether he would sell this property to the Lutherans. As he answered at once in the affirmative, the delegation took the liberty of informing him that the Reformed gentlemen had assured us previously he had not wanted us to have any part of the land, not even in common with the Reformed. All this Mr. Lawson, much surprised, fully denied; and thus the hidden intrigue of some of the Reformed members was revealed. We saw with great regret that there were people who could even begin divine service with envy and hatred, and that the old saying had again come to pass: Where a church for worship is built, there the devil builds a chapel."

A new difficulty arose when Mr. Lawson revealed that he was only willing to part with this lot provided five other lots adjacent to it were bought also. The least Lawson would sell his property for was 300 pounds Maryland gold, and that was considered a bargain. The little flock of Lutherans which had had trouble in raising the five pounds due the pastor who came to visit them, debated long whether they should enter into this contract, which meant that they would remain in debt for years to come. There were only a few among them who had even the modest fortune that would enable them to contribute; moreover the war was still on and things were uncertain.

At last, five members rose up and pledged to buy a lot apiece, each at great sacrifice. Mr. Lawson was informed that the congregation was willing to enter into a contract with him. "Accordingly we divided the whole lot into six parts, the first of them being the lot selected previously for the church building. From the front of this lot we cut off a portion for an approach to the church. The remaining five lots were laid out in accordance with the plan of the town." The largest parcel, reserved for the church, was a bargain, "but those who took the lots, out of regard for the congregation, paid the more." The names of those who agreed to buy the rest of the property have been handed down to us:

Charles F. Wiesenthal	Lot No. 119 for £	75
Conrad Conrath	Lot No. 120 for £	81
Caspar Grassmuck	Lot No. 121 for £	38
Wilhelm Hackel	Lot No. 122 for £	38
Moritz Wörschler	Lot No. 123 for £	38
The church lot thus was made as cheap as possible	£	30
	£	300

In 1758, three years after its organization, the Evangelical-Lutheran congregation of Baltimore had achieved what its leaders had hardly conceived possible at the outset: it had acquired land for its church out of its own means. The deplorable conflict with their Reformed brethren and the repeated congregational conferences before the land was bought, had welded the people together. Everywhere we can feel the influence that Pastor Bager's ministry had on the early development of their life as a church. The first election in the history of the Lutherans in Baltimore was held. Michael Tiefenbach was chosen as the first elder to guide the congregation during the absence of the pastor and to assist Moritz Wörschler, who had up to now done most of the work which the young congregation required. Although the building of a church could not be realized immediately, the congregation had the land on which to build it as soon as funds could be raised for the building materials.

Meanwhile, however, the successful campaign against the French had restored normal conditions in Pennsylvania and enabled Pastor Bager to resume his old charges. He had to inform the good people of the Baltimore congregation that he could no longer include them in his travel schedule, since "the journey of over sixty miles became too arduous for him" in addition to his already wide range of pastoral work. Another Lutheran clergyman had meanwhile settled in York County, Pennsylvania, where the congregations were constantly increasing. He agreed to visit the people in Baltimore when Bager discontinued his services there.

The first church facing Fish Street (now Saratoga)

On July 9, 1758, the Rev. Johann Caspar Kirchner presented his credentials to the elder of the Baltimore congregation. Still remembering the frequent visitations by charlatans and imposters, the congregation accepted Kirchner only after he "had given sufficient proof both of his character and also of the fact that he had already had charge of a congregation as an ordained pastor."

Pastor Kirchner likewise promised to come down from York every sixth week. His annual salary for preaching and administering Holy Communion was fixed at six pounds Pennsylvania gold. As the contracts with his other congregation in York County were originally drawn, only for one year, the Baltimore congregation also engaged Kirchner for one year. In July 1759, this contract was extended, since his services had proved very satisfactory.

After more than three years of saving and preparing, the congregation proceeded in 1762 with the construction of its first house of worship. The church lot was still largely unpaid for, but the increasing number of members made it impossible to continue worship service in private homes. The chronicler of the church expresses the joy and satisfaction of the people better than any historian could: "To their glory, be it known to posterity, our members although weak and few in number, still with much zeal endeavored to provide everything necessary for the erection of the church, and with concerted efforts began to build and in a short time completed the work. Accordingly, we had a church of our own without being exposed to further vexatious tricks which always would have disturbed us." The last remark reminds us that the relations between the Lutherans and the Reformed were still strained on account of the earlier conflict.

The little Lutheran church was a primitive structure upon the steep hill near Jones' Falls. It was approached only with difficulty, and the steep, sandy hill was very inconvenient for the older people. Nevertheless, the congregation had found its first permanent home, which was a monument to their honor and credit. Many years later, Pastor J. Daniel Kurtz reminded the people of Zion of the willingness to sacrifice which distinguished the congregation in 1762: "May our contemporaries remember these and similar sorrowful days of their forefathers, and thank the Lord in humility of the heart, if they in the actual wealth of their congregation can worship their God in well-constructed, beautiful temples." The old manuscript gives testimony of the fact that they were well aware of their limitations, when we read: "Wisely we had to cut our coat according to our cloth, and erected only a wooden building which we would consider a school-house until our revenues would allow us to build the church proper." But they were also looking forward to the future when the chronicler added: "If, however, a church with a steeple should be built upon the hill, it cannot help being seen afar and will make a fine appearance. For the time being it could not at all be compared with the temple of Solomon, except for our ardent zeal which made it possible that within a short time we could gather there for services."

When Pastor Kirchner held his first service in the church it was a day of happy thanksgiving. The flock, scattered and without a home a few years earlier, now gathered for the first time in a church of its own, built by the members with their own hands. The roughly hewn benches, the unadorned walls of weatherboard were far from providing a comfortable setting for divine services. But comfort was alien to these pioneers who gathered there even in the harsh winter days when the cold northwest wind would pierce through the thin walls. Schoolmaster Wörschler led the singing, uncouth and simple as it was, unaided by the music of an organ. Then Pastor Kirchner would stand before the simple altar, lead the congregation in a prayer and begin his sermon. He had no great zeal for liturgical worship and, he sometimes spoke of the liturgy as "the exercises preparatory to the sermon."

Most Lutheran services of those days were lacking in form and content. Thus, the people got used to a simple worship service, of which the sermon was the core on Sundays when no communion was offered.

By the end of 1762 Pastor Kirchner received a call to serve as resident pastor from Shuster's Lutheran Church in York County, where he could improve his material welfare, but where he would be too far away to attend to the congregation in Baltimore. In January 1763, he assumed his duties at Shuster's. The Rev. Bager again agreed to visit Baltimore. A number of Lutheran ministers had recently arrived from Germany and taken over charges which up to that time had been held by Bager, thus enabling him to take over the eight services a year at which Kirchner had officiated in Baltimore. Again he faithfully served the people whom he had assisted in their first organization, until he was called to New York.

Sunday services now became more frequent for the Baltimore congregation. Besides the contracted pastors, Kirchner and Bager, several itinerants who traveled with the authorization of the Lutheran Ministerium of Pennsylvania stopped by at Baltimore on their way south. In the summer of 1762, the Rev. John Christopher Hartwick visited the Lutheran congregations on his way from New York to Virginia. He stayed in Baltimore for a short while and preached to everybody's satisfaction, but declined to accept the offer of the congregation to remain as resident pastor. He was forty-eight years old when he came to Baltimore for the first time and was not bound to any congregation in particular. He had come to America from Germany as a chaplain in a German regiment employed by the English government against the French, had served with distinction under General Amherst, and had afterwards taken up missionary work among the German Lutheran settlers along the Hudson and Mohawk Rivers.

No matter what favorable offers the Baltimore congregation made him, "he said plainly that he was willing to stay as long as he should see that he was of use, but did not want to be bound by a contract and to remain anywhere against his will or conviction." Still, as he again passed through Baltimore on his way back from Virginia, where he had enjoyed the hospitality of Lord Fairfax, by whom he was highly esteemed, he stayed for some weeks; and several times thereafter he served the church, even for months. Nothing but severe winter weather could keep him from roaming about. Thus, a few years later, Hartwick happened to arrive in Baltimore when the cold season was setting in, and he decided to remain until spring.

Now the church had services every Sunday. The records which Pastor Hartwick kept during this time are lost, but from the annals of the congregation we can gather that almost 100 communicants formed the Lutheran Church of Baltimore at that time. For the first time English was preached in the humble house of worship. "He showed us that he was already well versed in the English language, preaching at times in English. He also had many English hearers. But one could see at once that he was German. However well he intended to do things, yet the Shibboleth was there," our chronicler relates. Ten years prior, the small band of Lutherans had been allowed to hold its meetings in the Anglican St. Paul's Church; now English people came to the Lutheran Church to hear a preacher who was widely known for his attainments. The winter over and traveling weather ahead, Hartwick bade farewell to his friends in Baltimore and went on his way; "it seemed as if the spirit of the wandering Jew had taken full possession of him, for in no case did obligations, however strong, bind him to the same people longer than six months," we read in a biography of this remarkable, restless servant of the Gospel, whose name can be found in the records of Lutheran churches from Maine to Virginia.

Probably upon the request of Pastor Kirchner, another preacher from York, Pennsylvania, presented himself to the congregation in Baltimore, but met with the disapproval of the parishioners: the Rev. Nikolas Hornell, a Swede. Although he had acquired a certain knowledge of German, his sermons were hardly understandable for a congregation which had become used to consider the sermon as the principal part of the service and naturally wished to understand the message of the pastor. His adherence to the more formal way of worship was strange to them, "besides, he was a 'hard' Lutheran as to every paragraph of the Augsburg confession," and because of these differences, he went his way. The church, however, was still hoping to find a pastor who would take residence in Baltimore and through his continuous and regular ministry give stability to the congregation. But the congregation was not kept waiting very long.

The news of Pastor Johann Caspar Kirchner's return to Maryland from Pennsylvania was received with great hope and joy by the church. The valuable contributions that the Rev. Kirchner had rendered to them half a decade prior were still remembered with gratitude by the people. Pastor Kirchner, however, had to dampen their joy. During the Christmas season of 1767 he had performed his last services at Shuster's Church in York County, and because of his age and condition of health decided to retire. In the Barrens, near Baltimore, he bought an estate where he settled in 1768 to enjoy a few years of rest from his tedious labors in the ministry. Upon the request of his old flock in Baltimore he agreed to serve them temporarily, admonishing them to find a younger man who would finally take full charge of the church. To be sure, Charles F. Wiesenthal turned to the Lutheran Ministerium of Pennsylvania for help in securing a pastor, but the only one who would have been available, the Rev. John Andrew Krug, in 1769, declined to come to Baltimore.

In spite of his previous resolution, Pastor Kirchner decided to yield to the entreaties of his faithful people in Baltimore, when he saw that no one else could be obtained. He moved to town, gave up the idea of a restful life on his farm, to which he would have been well entitled, and from now on served as their first resident pastor. The congregation allowed him a salary of £50 a year, "which in view of our small numbers was considerable," the annalist stated, but continued that it was hardly enough for the pastor. "He could hardly eat his fill. Yea, we have found him at times eating his bread with tears. He was poor, which made him shy and despondent. But he was thoroughly honest and attended to his sacerdotal office with dignity and without hypocrisy."

At once Pastor Kirchner presented to the congregation his plans for a reform of the organization of the church. Although we have seen that the devoted Charles Wiesenthal (but also others, among them Michael Tieffenbach and George Lindenberger) had cheerfully taken up a part of the burden which was connected with the life of the church, in particular relieving Master Wörschler from administrative duties to enable him to devote all his time and energies to the youngsters under his care, there was only one elected elder at the time, and his duties were not defined. Furthermore, the records of the church were kept on loose slips of paper, likewise the accounts. All these matters Pastor Kirchner was determined to take up and settle to the best of his abilities. Truly a great task ahead for a man who had just previously entertained hopes of retiring!

Although the congregation was firmly established, the fact that it had existed for fourteen years without any written rules and regulations had necessarily led to considerable disorder and neglect. Some eager members had acted on behalf of the church in certain matters without having consulted the congregation. Other tasks had remained undone because nobody wanted to take the responsibility on his shoulders, without proper authorization. Pastor Kirchner, now being the resident minister, also felt that it was best to have his own duties and responsibilities clearly defined at the outset of his work with a congregation which had so far never had a resident parson.

After some deliberations with leading members of the congregation, he composed the draft of the first constitution which the Lutherans of Baltimore were to have. On June 10, 1769, he read the fifteen articles to the full assembly of the congregation, and after it was formally accepted by all the people present, every male communicant who was of age subscribed to the same with his own hand. This first constitution, which is reprinted in full as Appendix A, is remarkable in several ways. Unlike other Lutheran Church constitutions of its day, it contains no statement regarding the faith which the congregation confessed. The "Augsburg Confession" is not mentioned; moreover the word "Lutheran" appears only once in the preamble with reference to the name of the congregation, "Evangelical Lutheran Church of this town." True, many pastors in those days did not have too much knowledge about how to draw up a constitution. The confessional character of their church was more or less taken for granted. There was no other Lutheran Church but that which had accepted the Augsburg Confession of Faith as its fundamental premise. We shall see in the discussion of constitutions that were adopted later that the early negligence was carried further until it was purposefully taken up to justify changes in the confessional character of Zion Church.

The preamble states that there had been much confusion in the congregation and that these regulations and articles were intended to secure order and regulate the lives of the members as Christians. Of utmost importance was the creation of the vestry. The one-person eldership of the early years had proved unsatisfactory, and from now on two deacons and trustees were to be elected every year to have "supervision over church order and discipline and over the members of the congregation and their conduct." Three, four or more members "of good faith and unblemished conversation," should be elected as permanent elders to assist the pastor in the administration of his office. Once a year a congregational meeting was provided, at which occasion the financial accounts should be examined and the new elections held. Extraordinary meetings of the entire congregation could be convoked by the pastor if he deemed them necessary.

Pastor Kirchner also insisted that communion records be kept. All members intending to take Holy Communion were to give their names to him at least one day before confession. He entered these

CHARLES FREDERICK WIESENTHAL
1726-1789

names in his communion record book, and only after having inquired into the conduct and Christian character of the applicants, would he admit them to communion. Minor offenses, such as enmity toward others, required that the persons in question should appear at least one week before Communion Sunday and be reconciled with each other. However, "those who through gross and shameful sins give offense to the Christian congregation shall be excluded from Holy Supper until they publicly do penance."

According to the constitution it was the pastor's duty to keep a record of all births, baptisms, and funerals. Thirty-five men signed the constitution, which Pastor Kirchner himself wrote into his parish register which he called the *Kirchen Archiv*.

Immediately after the acceptance of the constitution the congregation proceeded to elect its first complete vestry. It does not surprise us that we find several names among the members of the vestry which have figured prominently in the life of the church in prior years. George Lindenberger, Charles Wiesenthal, John Schrein, William Hackel, William Levely and Moritz Wörschler were the first elders elected in accordance with this constitution, and Jacob Brown and Frederick Cole were entrusted with the office of deacons.

Ledgers were bought for the bookkeeping of the church, in which the dues were recorded and balanced every year. These first ledgers, or "Day Books for the Evangelic Luthern (sic) Congregation," as they were called, give us a complete picture of the contributions of all members. Like other business records of that time, they were written in English, and the names of the members appear in their anglicized forms. From 1769 on, we encounter the handwriting of the various members of the vestry, faithfully recording the intake of every amount, however small.

The administrative business well attended to, the congregation could now turn to another task which was very dear to their hearts, to increase the efficiency of their school. Schoolmaster Wörschler, under whose care the youngsters of the Lutheran people had been ever since the congregation was founded, had far-flung plans The annalist shows how strongly the congregation felt the need for a good school when he writes "it is an incontestable fact that a good school education lays the foundation of our future happiness." However strong this desire was, the people simply had no money to improve the school. The debts for the church lot had still to be paid and, year after year, devoured all the funds that were raised through regular contributions. Thus, the members considered the idea of organizing a lottery, as some other churches had done successfully. After much discussion, Moritz Wörschler outlined the scheme.

Wörschler, as schoolmaster, did not feel strictly bound to denominational limits. His was the idea of a large school for the children of all Germans in Baltimore, and, not without having his own interest as the future headmaster of such a school at stake, he confided the lottery scheme to his Reformed friends, who received it with much enthusiasm. Instead of executing it together with the Lutherans, who had conceived the idea first, the Reformed went to work right away, made their lottery public and succeeded in realizing a large sum of money. The chronicler states with grief that when the Lutherans found out about it, "it was too late for us to undertake anything of the kind. All we had to do was to look on with dry mouth and forget our grief." Wörschler was exposed to much criticism for his rashness, and many thought that "it had not been done without premeditation."

By the summer of 1771 the ardently anticipated day had come when the elders of the church could report to the congregation that enough money had been collected to pay for the church lot and the interest thereon. In a little over thirteen years the faithful congregation had saved and sacrificed sufficiently to free the church from debt. Now preparations had to be made for the day when the trustees of the church would receive the deed and officially accept the title to the land on which the church stood. George Lindenberger and Charles F. Wiesenthal were put in charge of all details connected with the payment of the debts and the draft of the deed. Since Lindenberger offered to attend to the financial matters and to collect all amounts from those who had subscribed to pay their share, it was left to Dr. Wiesenthal to see to it that the deed be drawn in the best interests of the congregation.

So far, we have mentioned Dr. Charles F. Wiesenthal only in passing. We have learned that he came to Baltimore in 1755, the same year Pastor Bager took charge of the Lutherans in the town, and that he was a practicing physician. While the majority of the members of the Lutheran Church in Baltimore were humble people of limited education who engaged in crafts of various kinds, Dr. Wiesenthal brought with him an excellent schooling which he had received in Germany. He did not limit his activities to his professional work, but from the beginning took a cheerful and profound interest in the church which he had joined according to the faith of his fathers. After his arrival he adjusted to life in a small American town in a remarkable way. No wonder then, that he soon rose to a position of leadership among his brethren of the Lutheran faith. In 1769 we find him elected as a permanent elder of the church. It was only natural that to him fell the task of drafting the deed. The people had confidence in him, and he was already respected among the English population of Baltimore.

He was well informed about the confessional premises of the Lutheran Church. Although the aging Pastor Kirchner had not included any statements on the fundamental beliefs of the Church in the constitution, Charles Wiesenthal felt that it was absolutely necessary to include a concise statement of the character of the Evangelical-Lutheran Church in Baltimore in the deed, lest other groups, calling themselves "evangelical," might sooner or later lay claim to the property which the Lutherans had labored so hard for. Furthermore, the name of the congregation had to be considered for correct entry in the deed. Although the constitution did not contain the word "German," the church had commonly come to be called "German Evangelical-Lutheran Church." If the word "German" was in the deed, Wiesenthal realized that this could some day represent another serious threat to the title of the Lutheran Church.

We may, with some certainty, state that it was again he who wrote in the "Church Archives": "Daily experience taught us that our children, almost entirely, learned and understood the English language quicker and better than our German tongue, and, in the case of many, there was even reason to fear that the language would be lost entirely and the religion with it. Now to build a church for the propagation of our Lutheran religion for our children and children's children was our chief objective. It was, therefore, our duty to see that, in case this should happen, there should be no ill-considered clauses in the deed, by which our children would be subjected to unnecessary litigation and might even lose their share in the church."

Because of this consideration, Dr. Wiesenthal thought it wise not to mention the word "German" in the deed, for "there might be some who without any special love for religion and inclined to quarrel, might deny the right of using the English language to those who need it for their edification, under the pretext it had been stipulated that it was to be a German church, even if there were only ten Germans." George Lindenberger agreed fully with Dr. Wiesenthal's plan to avoid mentioning any language in the deed.

Both gentlemen consulted the other members of the vestry. When the schoolmaster, Moritz Wörschler, was approached, he at once opposed any such consideration. He interpreted Dr. Wiesenthal's suggestion as an attempt to make the entire church English. His agitation among the members of the congregation caused a complete uproar: "that it was a German church and should remain such!"

While the waves of discord were swelling high, the date for signing the deed had drawn near. As he could not expect the approval of the other members of the vestry, but on the other hand the deed had to be completed, Dr. Wiesenthal took it upon himself to draft its text according to his best conscience, fully aware of the responsibility which rested upon him. From the original of the deed in the Hall of Records in Annapolis we quote the essential paragraphs of the deed as executed on September 5, 1771:

"that is to say that all the said piece or parcel of ground shall be and continue to be a place of public worship for the Evangelic protestant Congregation of the unvaried Augspurg (sic) Confession of faith Commonly distinguished by the name of Lutherans and also a Burying place for said Congregation for the use of the High German Lutheran Inhabitants in Baltimore Town and their Descendants for ever who do or shall hold to the said Confession of faith. But whereas it may happen that the Children of the members of the said Congregation will in process of Time become more perfect in the English Tongue than in the German Language, it is hereby covenanted and agreed that whenever the Majority of the Members of said congregation shall deem it necessary, they may at any time introduce the English Language in Preaching, etc., still admitting the German tongue to be preached to these that do not understand the English if occasion requires (that is to say, who do or shall hold or continue to hold and Confirm to all Essential Articles of the Unvaried Augspurg (sic) Confession of faith, provided always that no person shall be deemed to belong unto the said Congregation until he has steadily attended the public worship of God in said Congregation for the Space of Twelve Months and shall have regularly Contributed towards the Support of the Ministry and other Charges of the same according to the usage of said Congregation. . . . ''

This deed was signed over by Alexander Lawson to Charles Wiesenthal, Moritz Wörschler, George Lindenberger, John Schrimm, William Hackel, William Levely, and Jacob Eichelberger.

The deed in its wording represents a perfect supplement to the Constitution of 1769, which neither mentioned the confessional character of the church nor defined who was to be considered a member. The similarity of the provisions which Dr. Wiesenthal entered in the deed to the usual provisions of the constitutions of well-established Lutheran Churches makes credible the supposition that Dr. Wiesenthal consulted either his pastor or, since the Rev. Kirchner was advanced in years and took little interest in the life of the congregation apart from his officiating at the services, other Lutheran clergymen.

Moritz Wörschler evidently did not let the matter rest with that. The church was shaken by many months of violent congregational battles. The conflict finally culminated in the resignation of Dr. Wiesenthal and George Lindenberger from their office as elders. Meanwhile reports of the discord in the Baltimore church had spread to other Lutheran congregations, and with apparent horror the Lutheran people of Philadelphia, York and Lancaster heard that two elders of the Baltimore church intended "to suppress the German language in the church and introduce by force the English language for it—in one word, to make our church English"! After their resignation both men were no longer allowed to associate with the congregation until such time as they should be exonerated of the charges.

Not until March 1772 did the vestry meet, in the absence of Moritz Wörschler, Jacob Eichelberger and Jacob Brown, to restore the peace of the congregation and belatedly approve the action of Dr. Wiesenthal and his friend, George Lindenberger, who faithfully stood by him during these months of trial. The resolution of the truncated vestry was written into the records of the church:

"To put an end to the aforegone quarrel we the undersigned and the other elders of the congregation have according to our duty fully investigated matters and do not find the slightest foundation for the above charges against Mr. Lindenberger and Mr. Wiesenthal. According to our conscience and our belief we find them not guilty.

Elders: Johannes Schrimm
Wilhelm Hackel
Wilhelm Löble
Deacon: Friedrich Kohl.   March 23, 1772"

Our annalist very aptly and with much foresight added to the record: "If this happens now for the mere sake of a deed, what will happen in case it should actually be necessary? And this was a clear and true instance that an opinion, originating from stubbornness, once held by people, will infatuate them and make them forego a vital interest, not considering that their actions have bearing upon posterity."

During all this trouble, old Pastor Kirchner faithfully served his quarrelsome flock. After all, the congregation had somewhat increased, and instead of spending his final days peacefully on the farm which he had bought in 1768, he saw himself faced with an ever-increasing task. We do not find him involved in the matters that shook the congregation and almost led to the loss of two of its most outstanding lay leaders. He fulfilled his pastoral work, preached, and admonished the people to keep peace; he baptized and confirmed, he served them at the table of the Lord and buried many of the men and women who had laid the foundation for the church twenty years earlier.

It is a sad fact that while many of the details of the quarrel have been preserved and carefully recorded in the chronicle of the church, no hand has written down the date of the death of the good old man, who must have died with his boots on. After the culmination of the conflict we miss the familiar handwriting which we attribute to Dr. Wiesenthal's genius. Only here and there was an entry made, and we have to turn to other sources. Although we cannot say with certainty when Pastor Kirchner died, we assume that it was toward the end of 1772 or during the early part of 1773. "And though he was poor, he strictly observed his duties, punishing fearlessly the vices which came to his knowledge, and instead of making enemies for him, this only increased his authority, and he received now and then favors from friends who were convinced of his sincerity," is the only tribute that his congregation paid him.

The first storm had passed over the church. It left a congregation, though finally reunited by the formal action of some of its elders, marred by the scars of discord. The conflict was of a fundamental nature. On the one hand stood Moritz Wörschler, the eager, stubborn teacher of the old school, who had devoted his life to the language of the fathers, to whom German was everything. He had his following, and we may not be mistaken in believing that he had most of the congregation behind him. On the other hand stood Charles F. Wiesenthal, the enlightened, well-educated physician who looked forward and was well aware that, unless something unforeseeable should happen, the days that the church would remain purely German could be counted. Dr. Wiesenthal was widely acclaimed, and the congregation felt deeply indebted to him. When he was finally exonerated it was certainly due more to his standing and his personality than to the action which he had taken in connection with the deed.

The constitution, only three years old, had proved insufficient. But before a new one could be adopted, there had to be defined who was actually a member of the church and could vote on a new constitution. There was no provision regarding membership in Pastor Kirchner's basic regulations for the church. The church building itself was in need of repair. The owner of the adjacent grounds, a Mr. Harrison, had dug away the greater part of the hill on which the church was situated. Never before had the plight of the congregation been greater than in the days when Pastor Kirchner died and left the church without the leadership that alone could provide a way out of the dilemma.

When Pastor George Bager left Pennsylvania and at the same time discontinued his visits in Baltimore, he had accepted a call to the Lutheran church in New York. In 1767, a close friend of his, the Rev. John Siegfried Gerock, relieved him of his duties in New York, and he returned to Pennsylvania. Pastor Gerock had undoubtedly heard about the young church in Baltimore. Early in 1773 he was informed that the charge in Baltimore was vacant. Upon his inquiry the vestry of the church extended a call to him, which he accepted at once, glad to leave New York, where he had encountered many troublesome spirits. He wrote a letter to the council of Christ Church in New York in which he stated that he had accepted an honorable call from an Evangelical German congregation in the newly founded city of Baltimore, and now desired to resign his office in Christ Church. His resignation was accepted, and during its 26th Convention the Ministerium of Pennsylvania approved of his accepting the pastorate in Baltimore. He assumed his work on May 1, 1773.

For the first time in its history, the church in Baltimore was fortunate enough to engage a pastor who came to his office in the prime of his years (Pastor Gerock was 45 years old when he assumed his pastorate), full of plans and willing to build up a congregation which he knew had been neglected by the Ministerium for some time. What he found when he came to Baltimore was not too encouraging: strife within, the elements from without, and the digging neighbor. But for a man of his calibre it seemed an ideal task.

Pastor Gerock, with John George Bager and John Nicolas Kurtz, belonged to the leading group of Lutheran clergymen around the powerful figure of the patriarch, Henry Melchior Muhlenberg, who had organized the Lutheran Church in America. In 1752 the Lutherans in Lancaster, Pennsylvania, had forwarded a petition to the Consistory of the Lutheran Church in Württemberg, requesting that a minister be sent to America. The Consistory selected Pastor Gerock, a scion of a distinguished family of clergymen, to go and serve the Lutherans across the ocean.

Twenty-one years later, after his arrival in Baltimore, his first step was to give the church the new form of organization which it badly needed. In order to be impartial, and without waiting for the election of a new vestry, which would probably have revived

Kurze
Kirchen-Verfassung
vor
die Evangelische Lutherische
Gemeinde
in Baltimoretown
Wie sie zu der Zeit
Vor nöthig befunden, und
abgefaßt worden.
D. 10ₜₑ Jung 1769.

Im Nahmen der Allerheiligsten Dreyeinigkeit
Amen.

First Page of the Constitution of 1769

Signers of the Constitution—1773

the old strife, he deemed it best to entrust the seven members who were designated as trustees in the deed and the two elected deacons with the revision of the constitution. Thus he accomplished what had seemed impossible a year before: Dr. Charles Wiesenthal and Moritz Wörschler, George Lindenberger and Jacob Brown, and the others who had taken sides in the past conflict were peacefully engaged in rewriting the constitution for their church.

At first glance the outcome of their work looked like a compromise. The name of the congregation was clearly defined as "Evangelical High German congregation," and the "Augsburg Confession" was not mentioned. In reality, however, this new constitution embodied everything Wiesenthal and his supporters had stood for. Of the twelve articles, the seventh actually was the most important one. It read: "All members of the congregation who, *in accordance with the terms of the deed,* want to have rights in the church and to its property, the church-yard, and other privileges, must voluntarily pay proportional dues towards the maintenance and support of the church, justly and honestly."

With this provision the deed became a part of the basic law of the church. The growth of the congregation is mirrored in the fact that three additional elders were to be elected, one of the elders henceforth to be designated as the treasurer of the church. From now on, several new deacons were to be elected. The recent difficulties were reflected in Article 4, which provided that all justified complaints arising in the congregation should be kept within the church and not "spread about in town or country."

This second constitution was accepted by the congregation on August 5, 1773, and signed by 145 adult male members, and two Englishmen for their German wives, who were members. Only seventeen of these men were ignorant of writing and made their crosses, among them old Vitus Hartweg, the harness-maker whom we encountered at the very beginning of the congregation.

Now the time had also come when a new building could be erected instead of the ramshackle wooden structure which for over ten years had served both as church and as schoolhouse. The lumber recovered from it was sold to the highest bidder and a new brick building erected, offering sufficient space for the congregation at that time. From the very beginning this new structure was considered only a temporary house of worship until the increase of the congregation and the accretion of funds would warrant the erection of a permanent church.

After the new constitution was adopted, Pastor Gerock could proceed to consolidate the congregation, which had been considerably disturbed by the controversy over the wording of the deeds. It was as if the right man had come at the right time. New immigrants had come in great numbers, and many found their ecclesiastical home with the Lutheran congregation in Baltimore. The clouds on the political horizon did not remain without effect on the Lutherans of Baltimore. The resistance against measures of the British colonial authorities, growing as it was all along the Atlantic seaboard, found considerable support among the German Lutherans. Although the British church tax seems not to have caused any immediate difficulties, the Lutherans were quite willing to become freed from the financial burden and also from the tutelage of the Anglican Church, for which they paid without receiving anything in return. Most Lutheran congregations (there were fifteen in Maryland on the eve of the Revolution) had developed into strong, active groups. The revolt against English rule would not only bring them equal rights with the Anglican Church, which had so far been the dominant church, but would also offer the Germans a chance to take an active part in the political and civic life of Baltimore.

Thus, our Lutheran congregation in Baltimore had gathered enough explosive spirits when the war came. The call to arms was immediately answered by the youth of the congregation. The "German Company," formed in 1776, the Rifle Company, and many other Maryland units show familiar names on their rosters. The "German Company" was almost the Lutheran Church's own. Out of nine officers, six were young men from the congregation: Samuel Gerock, Peter Mackenheimer, Christian Mayer, John Lindenberger, John Mackenheimer, and George Cole. Samuel Gerock, son of the pastor, was permitted to enlist by his parents only with much apprehension, because his younger brother Sigfried Henry had just died at the age of sixteen from an illness.

While the youth left for the battlefields, the older members of the congregation took their places on the home front. We find Barnet Eichelberger and George Lindenberger on political committees. Lindenberger manufactured considerable amounts of powder for the army. Engelhard Yeiser, expressly cited for his patriotic attitude, supplied the militia with meat. Everywhere we find familiar names. Men and women who had been regarded as "foreign immigrants" by their English neighbors now bore with them the burden of the war which was to bring freedom to all of them. Space forbids listing the many contributions to the war effort by the Lutherans of Baltimore, but one man in particular should be remembered whose part was of eminent importance in Maryland to the successful conduct of the war: Dr. Charles Frederick Wiesenthal. The public offices that he held during the war years are innumerable. From the beginning he was in charge of the general supervision of medical affairs. He was appointed surgeon-general of the Maryland troops. For years he supervised the medical equipment for the army. Unforgotten is his appeal in the "Maryland Gazette" of March 12, 1776:

"Our repose which we have hitherto enjoyed, in preference to our neighboring Colonies, is at last disturbed; and we are now called forth to our defense. The alacrity with which our brave countrymen assemble, and the determination to fight, visible in every countenance, demonstrate that if the enemy should be hardy enough to encounter them, we have reason to expect some wounds. The necessity of taking all imaginable care of those who may happen to be wounded (in their country's cause) urges us to address our humane Ladies, to lend their kind assistance in furnishing us with linen rags, and old sheeting for bandages, &c. to be delivered to Dr. Wisenthall (sic!) or any member of the Committee."

Pastor Gerock guided the congregation during the war years. He shared the anxieties, and the joy over the final victory. But many things had remained undone. The country, now no longer ruled by Britain, became, increasingly, a haven for those seeking freedom from want and freedom to earn and live. Many of the German immigrants still came as so-called redemptioners. The practice of indenturing people for the price of their passage was often used as a cloak for the utmost cruelty and injustice. How painful it was for Pastor Gerock when a young couple came to him to be married and he was obliged under law to make sure that neither of the parties was still indentured to someone. This meant that he could not perform the marriage rites unless the master of the indentured person gave his written consent. Time and again these indentured servants brought justified complaints to him, but there was no legal protection for these people.

Soon after the war, Dr. Charles F. Wiesenthal and Christian Mayer of the Lutheran congregation and other prominent Germans decided to form a society for the protection of German and Swiss immigrants who might land in Baltimore. For many years this society, the German Society of Maryland, intervened when cases became known in which ship captains and masters took brutal advantage of immigrants.

Freed of the burden to pay the annual tax to the Anglican Church, the Lutherans could now devote all of their means to their own church. First of all, the salary of the Pastor was raised from 100 pounds a year to 160 pounds, and after the war the Rev. Gerock received an annual compensation of 200 pounds from his congregation.

The house of worship could no longer hold the much-increased congregation. In 1785 an addition was built which was considerably larger than the house itself. A special dedication ceremony was prepared for the Sunday on which the congregation was to use the newly enlarged church for the first time. A young student of theology, who had just entered the ministry and upon the request of the Lutheran Ministerium was making a missionary tour to vacant congregations and scattered members of the Lutheran Church in Virginia and Maryland, happened to pass through Baltimore on his way homeward to Pennsylvania. He called to see the Rev. Gerock, who was so gratified to see the son of his valued friend, the Rev. Nicolas Kurtz, that he requested the young Daniel Kurtz to stay for the dedication services and fill his pulpit for that special occasion. Daniel Kurtz cheerfully acceded to this proposal and preached on the day when the newly enlarged building was committed to its purpose.

After Daniel Kurtz had returned home, Pastor Gerock, who was then very weak and feeble, wrote a letter to the Rev. Nicolas Kurtz expressing the desire to have young Daniel come to Baltimore for one year to assist him in his ministerial duties. With the consent of his father, Daniel Kurtz left immediately for Baltimore and assumed the duties which Pastor Gerock assigned to him: to preach on Sunday afternoon, visit the parochial school and instruct the children.

The year 1785 is of great importance in the history of the Lutheran congregation. Since the time when the Rev. Siegfried Gerock had taken over the congregation, in May 1773, contact with the Synod of Pennsylvania had been lost. Gerock, although bound by personal friendship to many prominent members of this Lutheran body, had kept aloof from the synodical connection. On May 23, 1785, the members of the Ministerium at their annual convention at Philadelphia were very much surprised to receive a communication from "Zion's Church in Baltimore City." Here for the first time we encounter the name "Zion" for the church in Baltimore. Now, since the congregation had a large building which would suffice for many years, it accepted the glorious name of "Zion" of which the psalmist sang: "Let Mount Zion rejoice, let the daughters of Judah be glad, because of thy judgments. Walk about Zion, and go round about her: tell the towers thereof." Proudly Zion Church stood on the hill, crowned by a little tower, overlooking the city of Baltimore.

The communication to the Ministerium, by the way, expressed a concern on the part of the people of Zion which proves that at last their interest in the whole church was revived. Pastor Daniel Schroeter of Hanover, Pennsylvania, had for several years visited scattered Lutherans west of Baltimore. His personal conduct was of much concern to Zion's people. The Ministerium investigated the matter, and upon a second complaint from Zion in 1787, Pastor Schroeter was finally found guilty of "drunkenness, lying, shameful hypocrisy and sordid stinginess." He repented and the convention forgave him.

Meanwhile, Daniel Kurtz had taken up his duties. He soon became a favorite in the congregation, and a great many of the members desired him to perform pastoral labors for them. This very naturally gave offense to the senior minister, who, at the expiration of the year, let his assistant understand that his services could now be dispensed with altogether. Mr. Kurtz accordingly preached his farewell sermon, telling the people that, the time having passed for which he had been engaged, he would return home, and entreated them to remain united and to live in harmony.

His departure, however, caused a split in the congregation. Without consulting Pastor Gerock and his supporters, the vestry and several other members sent a letter to Daniel Kurtz, urging him to return to Baltimore. At the same time the Synod received a letter from the congregation, in which the Ministerium was requested to ordain the Rev. Daniel Kurtz as its regular preacher. The Ministerium considered the matter, decided that the congregation in Baltimore was a rightful member of the Synod and submitted to Daniel Kurtz some questions to be answered in writing instead of a formal examination, in order to speed up his return to Baltimore.

When Kurtz arrived, Pastor Gerock refused him the use of Zion Church. Without hesitation, the Rev. Kurtz and his friends left Zion Church, secured the use of a Methodist Church, and held their services apart from the old congregation. In a public meeting the dissenters elected their own vestry, consisting of the elders Johannes Leypold, Engelhard Yeiser, Carl Gärts, Friedrich Kohl, Peter Frick, Johannes Schrimm, and Carl Schwartz and the two deacons, Philipp Wehner and Friedrich Reinhart.

The old congregation consisted of a small flock, mostly of older members who remained faithful to Pastor Gerock and did not share the opinion of Pastor Kurtz and his followers that Gerock had neglected his duties and had conducted the affairs of his church contrary to views held by the Synod. A document was drawn up in favor of Pastor Gerock, stating that "those that have taken no part in the split and do not recognize that there is anything of right in the complaints against their Pastor Gerock, but rather are satisfied with him in every way, do voluntarily endorse him by subscribing their names. And whereas they continue to hold services regularly and whereas they are in possession of the church which even many of them helped to found, and have, according to its statutes, observed friendship, these constitute the real congregation."

On March 18, 1787, the continuing congregation elected its own vestry. Dr. Wiesenthal, John Tinges, Jacob Brown, Peter Littig, Henry Ganz, and Johannes Breitenbach were elected elders, and Samuel Mayer and George Levely, deacons. The Rev. Gerock was confirmed as the sole minister.

The split seemed to be considered permanent. But again it was Dr. Wiesenthal who was unwilling to see the congregation to which he had devoted so many years of faithful service divided forever. He approached Pastor Kurtz, and after a conference both men let it be known that a reunion could take place. Pastor Gerock, who was known to his brethren of the *Ministerii* of Pennsylvania and New York as a hard man to deal with and who had caused many a rift by his independent actions, finally consented to readmit Pastor Kurtz and his congregation.

On Easter Sunday 1787, Zion was reunited again. Both pastors preached to a flock which had never before been so large. It was decided to draw up articles of reconciliation, and a week later, on April 3, 1787, both pastors signed a document in the presence of Charles F. Wiesenthal of the Gerock congregation and Peter Frick of the Kurtz congregation, exhorting both factions to follow their example.

Pastor Kurtz, with the help of Dr. Wiesenthal, insisted on a number of points to be added to the constitution. Among these, the following ones were of importance:

> *Membership* was once again clearly defined in accordance with the terms of the deed.
> The *constitution* was to be read publicly once a year.
> *Baptismal records,* which so far had never been kept, should be entered in a regular book, likewise all *marriages* and *burials.*
> Both *pastors* were to share all duties, i.e. one preaching on Sunday morning, the other one in the afternoon. *Confirmation* was to be administered jointly, according to the use and stipulation of the *Augsburg Confession.* Likewise the *Holy Supper* was to be administered jointly; the old pastor offering the bread, the junior preacher the chalice.

The stipulation of the agreement that both pastors "should by virtue of their office offer to the congregation a model of composedness, meekness and humility" did not apply for long, for on October 25, 1787, Pastor Gerock died, 61 years old, a broken and deeply wounded man. In later years, Pastor Kurtz expressed sorrow over his rash and youthful actions, but he felt that the interests of the church had demanded of him the stand he took. Dr. Wiesenthal, whose work as a layman had such a deep influence on his church and who had brought about the reunion of the congregation, was also laid to rest three years later. With him the last one of the early members was gone. A youthful congregation and a young and enterprising pastor constituted Zion Church on the eve of a triumphant growth.

During the early years of the pastorate of Pastor Kurtz the communion vessels were acquired which are still in use today. They were made by Lewis Buichle, a well known German silversmith and a member of Zion, who came to the United States about 1798. The flagons are marked with his initials. These communion vessels, older than one-and-a-half centuries and revered by many generations of Zion Church members, are highly treasured witnesses to the continuity of Zion's history.

JOHANN DANIEL KURTZ
1785-1833

CHAPTER TWO

A New Leader and His Successors

Pastor Gerock's death committed the congregation to the sole leadership of the youngest permanent pastor whom Zion ever had. Born in 1763 in Germantown, Pennsylvania, J. Daniel Kurtz was in his twenty-fifth year when he found himself suddenly confronted, alone, with the manifold problems of his church. Some of the bitterness of the old feud remained even after the death of the old minister, and much of the fine groundwork that Pastor Gerock had laid during the thirteen years of his service at Zion had deteriorated during the fight that he and his hard-boiled followers had put up against the young man who shared his pulpit.

Youthful Daniel Kurtz represented a new generation of Lutheran clergymen. He was one of the first American-born pastors to be ordained. He was German in language and customs, but American in heart and spirit. The experiences of his youth were different from those of the pastors who had served Zion so far. He had not emigrated from the Old Continent. He had not had to adjust to an entirely new environment. He was born into it.

His educational experiences are typical of the schooling available in his days. When he was six years old, his father sent him to a German schoolmaster in Tulpehocken to acquire basic training in reading and writing. After 1771, when the family moved to York, he pursued his studies under the direction of his father, the Rev. John Nicolas Kurtz, one of the pioneers of the Lutheran Church in America, who had immigrated in 1745. In his father's home many prominent clergymen were welcomed as guests, especially during the war, when the Chaplain of Congress, Bishop White, made his home with the Rev. Kurtz. Congressmen and ambassadors were accommodated, and meeting them provided much inspiration for the diligent student. Very early in his life Daniel Kurtz had felt the urge to become a minister as his father was. He describes the growth of this desire in his autobiography: "This feeling was indeed vague and indefinite, and wholly inexplicable to myself, but still the general idea took hold of my mind, that I must preach the Gospel. Whether my father was aware of this, and whether this had any influence in determining him to devote me to the ministry, I cannot possibly say."

His father soon felt, as formal schools such as a seminary for Lutheran students of theology were not yet established, that it would be best to commit his son to one of his most learned friends, Dr. Henry E. Muhlenberg of Lancaster, for instruction in the classical languages and in theology. Dr. Muhlenberg gave his young scholar much opportunity to share in his own activities, which also included natural sciences, as he was at that time justly regarded as one of the best naturalists in the United States. He did not attempt to impose knowledge on Daniel Kurtz, but kept the formal lessons to a minimum. "But my teacher soon told me that I must learn to help myself, while he gave me the free use of his library, and liberty to occupy the room as the place of my study. His collection of books was, fortunately, large and judicious, one of the best then in this country." This method of diligently acquiring much knowledge of classical culture, languages and sciences through his own reading was kept up by Daniel Kurtz throughout his career and accounts largely for his well-rounded knowledge, which astonished people with whom he came in contact.

For a while he entertained hopes of studying in Germany for two or more years. Professor J. David Schoepf of Jena, who spent some time with Dr. Muhlenberg, was willing to take young Kurtz along to Jena and instruct him in medicine, while the well-known theologian, Dr. Lesz, would prepare him for the ministry. His father, however, declined his request to depart for Europe, because he felt that the church in America urgently needed young men like him and "that I could learn just as much where I was as in Europe."

After concluding his studies in Lancaster, he presented himself for examination to the Synod of Pennsylvania, held in Philadelphia in 1784, and was licensed to preach for one year. At first he assisted his father in preaching, in catechizing, and in visiting the sick in York. With his brother-in-law, the Rev. J. Goering, he was appointed to visit the Lutherans in Virginia and Maryland. The following year he repeated the trip and on that occasion preached in Baltimore. On June 14, 1786, he was ordained by the President of the Synod, the Rev. Dr. Helmuth, in Zion Church in Philadelphia.

The position of a pastor at Zion Church in Baltimore was ideal for a young man of his age. First of all, the synodal contact had to be fully re-established, since Pastor Gerock had turned the church away from the Synod. For Daniel Kurtz the Synod was a vital part of the life of the church. The synodal meetings with prominent pastors and laymen from all over the Lutheran Church, with their discussions and lectures, sermons and exchanges of experience, were a source of inspiration to him in his younger years and a platform from which to present the interests of his congregation in particular, and the needs of the whole church in general, throughout his ministerial career.

In 1789 his father, Pastor Nicolas Kurtz, having retired from his office at York, moved to Baltimore and assisted his son for five years with his wise counsel, derived from long experience. At various times he preached on Sundays when his son was on calls to other Lutheran churches on request of the Synod. In 1794, Nicolas Kurtz, the *Senior ministerii Lutherani,* died and was buried in the garden of Zion Church.

Everything at Zion was well in order now. The records were kept with great care. Baptisms, communions, marriages, confirmations and burials were meticulously recorded by Pastor J. Daniel Kurtz. His successful work soon became known to other churches. The Lutherans of Alexandria, Virginia, offered him their pastorate. Hagerstown and Georgetown extended calls to him; the church at Lebanon, Pennsylvania, implored him to take charge of its large congregation; but he remained faithful to his task in Baltimore, firmly convinced that his duty was to remain there.

Much of his time was devoted to the school. He extended the German School and took over most of the instruction. The catechumens were solely under his guidance. At first he confirmed one class every three years; from 1793 on, every two years. On the fifth Sunday after Trinity in 1787, his first class of forty-five confirmands partook of the Holy Communion; in 1790 he had fifty-three confirmands. The Holy Supper was regularly offered three times a year, on Easter, Whitsunday, and around Christmas. In 1797, after he had engaged Adam Gottlieb Rabb as teacher, Pastor

Kurtz could report to the Synod that Zion Church had opened the first English Lutheran School alongside the German School, to accommodate children of Lutheran parents, who were ignorant of the German language.

When Kurtz came to Baltimore he was unmarried. The church had no parsonage, and he lived most of the time with members of the congregation. But in the spring of 1790 he announced to his people that he had chosen a girl of the congregation, Maria Messersmith, to become his wife. This announcement, which came without too much surprise to many, at once was met with the decision of the congregation to build a parsonage. In April 1790, the church trustees bought the ground for that purpose from James Sloan. The deed provided "that the said piece of ground with improvements thereon, shall forever hereafter be and continue as a parsonage house for the Evangelic Protestant Congregation of the High German Lutheran Inhabitants of Baltimore Town, and descendants forever, who shall hold the Augsburg Confession of Faith." The building was soon afterwards completed, and on September 5, 1790, the happy couple moved in.

The pastor's wife at once began a fruitful activity among the poor and needy of the German population in Baltimore. There was no public welfare at that time, and to the church alone was left the task of caring for the poor. In 1800, Zion Church was incorporated for the first time, as the state laws required then, and received its share of alms from public funds for distribution among its needy members.

Subscriptions for enlarging the house of worship were likewise taken up, and in 1795, Pastor Kurtz ordered an organ for the church. The famous Moravian organ-builder, David Tannenberg of Lititz, Pennsylvania, was entrusted with the order and delivered an organ in 1796, which remained in the use of Zion Church for 44 years. Although we have no description of it, we can deduce from its cost of $600 that it was a rather elaborate piece of work for those days. Schoolmaster Adam Rabb was Zion's first organist.

The pastor extended his ministry also to Lutherans living in the country. Many people who lived far away began to appear in church for the communion services. Although Baltimore was constantly growing, the conditions were far from ideal in the city. The great number of immigrants who had settled there, the unhealthy climate, which many of them were not used to, caused much disease and death. The rate of infant mortality was especially frightening even for those days. In the decade from 1787-1796, 402 members of the congregation died; of those, 184, almost one half, were children under four years of age. From 1797 until 1806, the church lost 611 members through death, again 245 children under four among them.

Pastor Kurtz and his wife lost several of their eleven children in infancy, and his faith alone consoled him in those sorrowful years when he wrote: "I consider all children as saved who die in their innocence; nevertheless, I have felt how painful it is to parents to follow their offspring to the grave, though we know to die is gain to them, and that after death they quickly mature to the happy state of holy angels. I believe that many adult persons, with all their pious wishes, by tottering, falling and rising, and with all their endurance, scarcely attain to a child's salvation."

Throughout the Lutheran Church in the country, the growth and development of Zion in Baltimore was observed with much interest and satisfaction. At one of the gates of immigration, the Baltimore church was fulfilling its natural vocation of gathering those who came to the land from German-speaking countries and giving them a harbor where the faith of their fathers had taken deep roots in the new soil. In 1796 Pastor Kurtz on behalf of the vestry invited the Synod of Pennsylvania to hold its next meeting in Baltimore. Although this venerable body had never convened in Baltimore before, always having considered the Lutheran Church there as one of the infant churches of the Lutheran faith, the invitation was accepted, an action expressing the conviction of the church leaders that Zion in Baltimore now would rank among the larger churches of the Synod. On Sunday, June 11, 1797, the Synod met in Baltimore. Pastor Kurtz had approached the two other German churches, the Reformed and the United Brethren, and they wholeheartedly extended the hospitality of their homes to the Synod delegates. Dr. Helmuth of Philadelphia, Dr. Henry Muhlenberg, Rev. Jacob Goering, and many other leading Lutheran clergymen preached in nine services during the three days of the convention. The clergy of the Ministerium and the lay delegates stayed in the homes of many members of the congregation. These were three jubilant days for Zion, and the grateful Synod sent a message to

Zion's people thanking them for "the remarkable hospitality of the congregation at Baltimore."

For the first time the whole congregation had witnessed the proceedings of the Synod. Pastor Kurtz was happy to have found this opportunity to acquaint all his people with the church body embracing most of the Lutherans in America. This day was a very important factor in his further work of making Zion an integral part of the Synod. It also helped to deepen the relationship with the Reformed and United Brethren congregations. Already in 1796 the Reformed Church, which had been destroyed by a flood, had been rebuilt with the generous help of the Lutherans. Pastor Kurtz had led the congregation out of his church to the scene of the disaster, preached on the ruins of the Reformed Church and taken up a collection. When the cornerstone of the new church was laid, he offered the prayer. Under his leadership Zion became more than ever community-conscious, and the days when Lutherans and Reformed were involved in petty quarrels were altogether forgotten.

When Pastor Daniel Kurtz led the people of Zion into the new century, the pioneer days for the Lutheran Church in Baltimore were finally over. Sons had taken the places of the founding fathers. Emigration from Germany suddenly died down to a trickle as a result of the European wars. The city of Baltimore had grown to more than 40,000 inhabitants with an export trade volume of more than $15,000,000 in merchandise per year, thus becoming the third largest port of the young American Republic. Zion had grown with its city. In 1794, the pastor had recorded 162 communicants; in 1795, there were 283; in 1804, Zion Church had 318 communing members. Within one decade, the membership had doubled. In a single communion service, on Whitsunday of 1807, 195 communicants were counted. The once small flock of Lutherans in Baltimore had developed into a sizable congregation for which the old house of worship was becoming too small in spite of the large addition which had been built in 1785. The ever increasing number of baptisms at Zion seemed to insure the future strength of the Lutheran community. Every year, more than one hundred children were baptized into the church by Pastor Kurtz:

| 1800: 102 | 1801: 165 | 1802: 156 | 1803: 134 | 1804: 126 |
| 1805: 137 | 1806: 131 | 1807: 150 | 1808: 129 | 1809: 134 |

Altogether, a proud record of 1,364 baptisms within a period of ten years. Would there be room in Zion for all those whom he baptized? Pastor Kurtz was deeply concerned about those who would form Zion's congregation in less than a generation's time. Under a list of baptisms which he entered in the register of the church, he wrote this prayer: "O Arch-Shepherd Jesus! Receive all these souls into Thy flock, and keep them therein unto eternal salvation, for the sake of Thy death! This is the prayer of their teacher, Daniel Kurtz."

On June 5, 1803, Zion was again host to the Synod of Pennsylvania for its annual meeting. Again the pastor had to ask the other two German denominations in Baltimore to extend their hospitality to the synodal delegates, since his own church was too small to hold the meetings of the clergy and lay delegates of the Lutheran Church from far and near. Although the Reformed and the United Brethren gladly cooperated, Pastor Kurtz would much rather have received the leaders of his church in a new and larger Zion.

In the following years, he did not rest. His was the dream of a church which would not only be large enough for the congregation of his days, but also for that of generations to come. Knowing well the material limitations of his flock, he was patient in preparing his ambitious building program. True, a few of the members were quite wealthy, but most of them had little money to spare for anything apart from securing a moderate degree of prosperity for their own families. There were some outstanding businessmen of the city who were active members of his church: Philip Myers, a banker; Johann Machenheimer, the architect and builder; Johann Strobel and Henry Saumening, brewers and bottlers; Frederick Graf, a maker of leather goods; Frederick William Brune, J. H. Heidelbach, Daniel Diffenderfer and Peter Sauerwein, who were all engaged in wholesale and retail merchandising, and Peter Frick, a member of Baltimore's first City Council and attorney-at-law.

The pastor, however, knew that the building of a church could not be undertaken with two handfuls of well-to-do men alone, but would require the support and interest of the entire congregation. He preached to his congregation of the beautiful house of Zion and prayed to his Heavenly Father for His blessing. His prayers were answered, and his preaching fell on fertile ground. On Sep-

Zion Church 1808 to 1840—up to the fire

tember 15, 1806, the Church Council announced its decision to build a new church and called on the congregation: "As every member of this congregation will easily realize the necessity of a new church edifice, the Council again appeals to the liberality of the members who have proved their willingness to help on previous occasions. Donations from other friends of church institutions will be accepted with thanks and with a prayer that God may bless them abundantly in return. If this building should be begun the subscriptions may be paid in four installments." The subscription list was circulated, and in less than a year's time 273 individuals pledged $12,559.60, practically every communing member having answered the appeal of the Council.* In the same year, the lot on which the church was to be erected was bought for $8,600.

A busy time began for the pastor and Council of Zion. The architects, George Rohrbach and Johann Machenheimer, both church members, who were entrusted with the design of the church and the supervision of the numerous craftsmen who were constructing it, had to be consulted, informed and supervised. Early in 1807, the cornerstone was laid. The annual synodal meeting in Lancaster, Pennsylvania, had to be attended. Besides all regular services, Pastor Kurtz solemnized 64 marriages, officiated at 57 funerals and baptized 150 children during that year. All the work culminated in 1808. A class of 43 confirmands was to be accepted into the communion of the church. The number of communicants increased to 313. The Synod at Lebanon in Pennsylvania required his presence because he was to be elected secretary of the Synod for the year. He had to travel alone to the convention, since all the money was needed for the building fund. In previous years a member of the Church Council had always accompanied the pastor to represent Zion at the synodal meetings. Pastor Kurtz's regular duties in those days were in themselves of considerable dimensions. Many members lived at distant points. Since there were hardly any means of public conveyance, the pastor had to ride on horseback to visit the sick who lived outside of the city.

The work on the new church was nearing completion when fall arrived. The organ was transferred from the old church, adorned with wood carvings, and installed in the new building. The red brick

---

*The complete subscription list of 1806 is to be found on page 125 as Appendix D.

structure with the white trimmings was ready for use. On October 9, 1808, the great day had come of which the pastor had dreamed for a long time. The program of the service of dedication has been preserved. To the sound of a symphony played on the old organ, Pastor Kurtz could proudly lead the guest ministers, followed by the Church Council, into the new house of worship. Specially written texts adapted to melodies of Lutheran hymns and an Ode of Praise exuberant with joy upon Zion's completion were used for the singing of the congregation and of the choir during the three services on the day of dedication. The Church Council directed an appeal to the members, which, besides expressing overwhelming joy, revealed deep concern about the financial obligations in the future. But it also admonished the people of Zion not only to give silver and gold, but above all, to give their hearts. "The Church Council rejoices with you on this day and exclaims with deeply moved hearts: Behold the handiwork of the Lord! Now German Zion stands before us in its beauty! The Lord made you willing to contribute your share—you have done much, but you will certainly not hold back your generous hands, as the Lord has helped you so far. We are sure that you will reveal your joy in our Zion also in the future by increasing your contributions according to your abilities. It would be an expression of ingratitude to intimate the least doubt about your generosity on this memorable day. We are firmly convinced that you will offer your gift generously today to the glory of Him to Whom we are indebted for all that we possess. We still owe much, but we do not fear. We know your love, your patriotism, and your truly Christian attitude towards this House.

"One more thing dearest friends! You love your forefathers, you love the evangelical teachings; the truth of salvation as you learned it in your mother tongue is especially important to you. Do you want to do less for your children than your parents have done for you when they brought you up in their mother tongue? No! Without doubt you will not let that happen. Do not rest until your school affairs are on a foundation which will assure that this House also remains a House of God for your posterity, where the preaching will be in German and where the name of the Lord will forever be praised in this language."

There Zion stood and for the first time opened its gates to the congregation whose sacrifices had made the building possible.

> *Heavenly hosts sing Thy praise*
> *May also Zion's voices raise*
> *To Thee in all Thy magnitude*
> *Thy children's prayers—our gratitude.*

Thus began the Ode in the Sapphic style which, although rather crudely composed, expressed the feelings of the grateful people of Zion. The short square tower marking the Gay Street end of the sturdy brick structure contained a simple bell which would call the flock of Zion to service on happy and sad occasions. There were two entrances—one on Gay Street, and the other one on the south side of the building. Both had rounded Roman arches, while the windows were pointed in the Gothic style. An organ gallery extended across the east end of the church, and the pulpit at the west end was very high, reminding many a visitor of a "crow's nest" on top of a ship's mast. No wonder a legend persists among the people of Zion that once two stray sailors stumbled into the church on a Saturday night and on the next morning were found in the pulpit by Pastor Kurtz, seemingly feeling very much at home.

When the excitement over the dedication of the new church had passed, the pastor and his Council had to concentrate again on financial matters. The final bill of the building cost, which has been preserved, together with the price paid for the lot, exceeded by far the amount subscribed. (*see next page*).

New subscriptions were solicited, but from the beginning seemed inadequate. After the completion of the church, it became evident that the congregation owned considerable grounds which were no longer needed. The Church Council decided to sell as much of this land as could be spared, even after the building of a new school house, a parsonage, and a home for the teacher were projected. Meanwhile the old church continued to be used as a school house. The idea of selling ground, however, encountered considerable difficulties. The original deed of 1771 and also those of 1790 and 1793 provided that "all the said ground shall be and continue to be a place of public worship for the Evangelical Protestant Congregation of the unvaried Augsburg Confession of Faith." In order to enable itself to dispose of the unwanted ground, the Church Council appealed to the General Assembly of Maryland to

DETAILED COSTS OF NEW CHURCH

Boards, shingles, etc.	$ 5,002.77
2,638 bushels lime	991.17
Carpenter	8,728.11
Masonry	2,547.04
246 rods 11½ ft. of stone	394.80
Stones for steps	13.00
685,094 bricks of different kinds	4,808.45
Plasterer	531.79
Ropes	381.00
Sand	357.94
Stone-cutter	942.59
Timber for scaffold (396 pieces)	237.68
Blacksmith	633.42
Nails and all kinds of hardware	516.44
Glazier and painter	726.42
Different jobs	631.94
For moving organ to new church	238.05
Carving at the organ	48.50
Oil to paint church	55.18
Curtains and one box of candles	31.04
Glass from Herr Fries	266.50
Beams, copper, lead, etc.	36.80
White lead, brushes, beams, carts, beverages, etc.	57.69
	$28,250.69
For the lot whereon the church stands was paid	$ 8,600.00
Total	$36,750.69

absolve the trustees of Zion Church of this clause of the deeds only with respect to the property intended for sale. After consideration of the reasons for the request, the Assembly in its November session of 1811 passed "An act to authorize the sale and conveyance of certain property held in trust by the German Lutheran Congregation of the City of Baltimore."

Pursuant to this act the church sold, from 1812 until 1817, seven lots for a total consideration of $23,274, including two parcels which were conveyed to the city of Baltimore and later became the bed of Lexington Street between Holliday and North

Streets. Through these sales the treasury of the church was replenished, and by 1817, Zion was free of debt.

Services were not as convenient then as they are today. Zion being the only Lutheran church in the city and its environs, many members had to spend the better part of the day getting to church, attending the service and returning home. There is no evidence of any complaints by the pastor or the Church Council regarding irregularity of attendance. Communion records were carefully kept and reveal that most of the members attended the services during which the Holy Supper was offered.

As a loyal member of the Synod, Pastor Kurtz conducted his worship services with the liturgy *(Kirchen-Agende)* published by the Lutheran Ministerium of Pennsylvania in 1786. The original publication of the liturgy contains his name as the youngest (and the last one) on the list of pastors who accepted it as binding for their services. Among this venerable list of America's Lutheran clergy we find also the names of Nicolas Kurtz and of Zion's first pastor, J. George Bager. Daniel Kurtz was eminently conservative with regard to the *Kirchen-Agende*. He was hardly ever seen during the administration of his office without the little volume in his hand. Rare were the occasions when he would perform without his text. Creeds and confessions, in their proper place, he regarded as excellent things.

In 1818, he supervised the printing of the second edition of the *Kirchen-Agende* and its translation into English, both published in Baltimore.

Let us join Zion's congregation in one of its services.

Before taking their places in church, men would stand for a short prayer, holding their hats before their faces. Most families rented their pews for the entire year. The pew rent in the new church ranged from $10 to $3, as it had been in the old House. In 1811, when most of the debts which the church had contracted were paid for, the pew rents were lowered, ranging now from $8 to $3, but the Church Council announced expressly: "Members whose circumstances do not permit them to pay $3, pay whatever they can." The service itself was preceded by an organ prelude which began when most worshippers had taken their seats. Upon the last strains of the organ Pastor Kurtz would enter the church,

German Lutheran Church
now Independent Zion
Erected by the German Lutheran reformed Congregation. in N. Gay Street. open'd 1808. cost 37,000 Dollars
Rohrbach & Mackenheimer drch.

followed by the Church Council, and take his place in front of the altar. The choir sang a hymn or an ode followed by a hymn sung by the entire congregation. After that, the minister from the altar exhorted the people to confess their sins and led them in the confessional prayer, which closed with the triple Kyrie. Then came the second hymn, and this was followed by the salutation (The Lord be with you), the response, and the proper collect from the hymn book. After the reading of the epistle lesson, the principal hymn was sung, and then came the gospel lesson of the day. Next came the creed in verse, and again a stanza or two of the hymn. When the pastor went up to the high pulpit, the congregation arose, joined in the Lord's Prayer, and remained standing through the reading of the scripture text, which was a repetition of the gospel lesson. Kurtz was a vigorous, systematic, and earnest preacher. With regard to his sermons, one of his colleagues wrote: "He adhered all his lifetime to the old pietistic school, both in sentiment and arrangement, and could hold an audience in silence and perfect attention for an hour." At the close of his sermon the pastor offered the general prayer from the pulpit, and then came the votum (The peace of God, etc.). After the closing hymn he went back to the altar; there was another salutation, response, and collect, and finally the benediction, followed by another verse of the closing hymn. While the organ played the postlude, the pastor left the sanctuary and the congregation filed out through the two large doors.

For many years the singing of the congregation had been in a bad state, as it was in most German churches in the early days. The Marburg Hymn Book had been in use at Zion for many years, probably since the beginnings of the congregation. This was very fortunate, since the Liturgy of 1786 provided that liturgy and the Marburg Hymn Book should be used together in the services. The need for a new hymn book, however, arose in the course of time. The American congregations had adopted many hymns which were not contained in the old Marburg Hymn Book; whereas some of its hymns were not used at all. In January 1816, it was announced in Baltimore that Daniel Kurtz and the Reformed preacher, the Rev. Dr. Becker, were preparing a common hymn book for use in both churches, with the authorization of their respective synods. In 1817, this *Gemeinschaftliches Gesangbuch* was published in Baltimore. Within two years it went through four editions, one of the most successful publications of the time.

But Pastor Kurtz not only collaborated in composing the new hymn book, he also founded Zion's *Singe-Gesellschaft* to cultivate the musical interests of the young people, and to provide a choir and soloists for the service. Cantor *(Vorsänger)* Benjamin G. Walz helped greatly in improving the singing of the congregation, which had once been no more than a slow, unmusical uttering of notes.

In those days not only the singing would have disillusioned a modern worshipper. The heating of the large church, which was 99 feet x 75 feet, presented a considerable problem. In order to fill the building with heat, the wood stoves were placed as high as possible, the result being that the floor was never sufficiently heated and the feet of the people always cold. During the service, the sexton would regularly go around and stir the fire. For winter and evening services, candles could provide only an imperfect light. At least twice during the worship the sexton had to top the candles, standing on a step ladder. He would even ascend the pulpit and perform his duty there. It takes little effort to imagine the merriment audibly expressed among the younger worshippers in the house when the sexton accidentally would put out a candle or would have too much trouble with the stove.

Pastor Kurtz never introduced a Sunday School for the adult members of the congregation. In accordance with the old Lutheran tradition, he contented himself with giving a thorough training to his catechumens, based on Martin Luther's Catechism. The parish school provided old fashioned but solid instruction in the three R's, with special emphasis on the teachings of the church.

During all this time, while the pastor was carrying out an ambitious building program, he kept in close contact with the Synod. There was only one synodical convention that he missed during this period. Usually he was accompanied by a member of the Church Council at these meetings. Twice already, Zion Church had been host to the Synod of Pennsylvania for its annual conference. Thus, the people of Zion had developed a strong feeling of belonging to the whole church. It is a touching testimony to this allegiance that Peter Sauerwein presented $30 on behalf of Zion's congregation to the synodical treasury in 1809, when the finances at Zion were at their lowest ebb.

JOHANNES UHLHORN
1823-1834

Pastor Daniel Kurtz's work as a spiritual leader in the largest city of Maryland did not remain unechoed on the outside. In 1816, the University of Pennsylvania bestowed upon him the degree of Doctor of Divinity for his outstanding work as a clergyman. He was the first Lutheran pastor in Maryland ever to be thus distinguished. His excellent articles on Justification in the *Evangelisches Magazin* found wide acclaim. Thus acknowledged as a man qualified for leadership, he could begin to reach out successfully for an active part in the reorganization of the Lutheran Church as a whole, and pave the way for an end to the spiritual deterioration which had befallen many congregations in the country. He kept in close contact with the other Lutheran pastors in Maryland and northern Virginia, where the congregations had grown in numbers and the particular interest of the churches required a strong organization to prevent them from losing their denominational consciousness. Special conferences, although they were held occasionally in that region until 1817, could not perform the mission that a regular Synod would fulfill. Most of the conferences of the Mother Synod of Pennsylvania were held at distant places. The time was ripe for a separate organization for the churches in Maryland and Virginia. Pastor Kurtz, who was instrumental in the preliminary steps to this end, wanted to see the new Synod created in full harmony with the Pennsylvania Synod, of which he had been a faithful member ever since he entered the ministry. The simultaneous creation of a General Synod which would unite all bodies of the Lutheran Church in America seemed the best guarantee that the formation of the Maryland Synod would not be divisive or schismatic.

On Trinity Sunday, June 6, 1819, the Seventy-second Convention of the Pennsylvania Synod met in Zion Church in Baltimore. For the first time, new Zion received the leaders and delegates of the church. The attending pastors and lay representatives assembled in the parsonage and, led by the host pastor, went in procession to the church. The main business on the agenda of this meeting was to act on the proposed formation of a General Synod. The Synods of North Carolina and New York had requested to become members of such a central body. A committee of six was appointed, two of them being from Zion, Pastor Daniel Kurtz and John Schorr, a member of Zion's Church Council. Their draft of a plan for the creation of the General Synod met with the approval of a majority of the delegates. The walls of new Zion resounded with hymns of praise and gratitude. Now Pastor Kurtz and his co-workers could proceed to rally the Lutheran churches in Maryland and Virginia into a separate synod, which would subsequently become a member of the General Synod.

On October 11, 1820, the clergy and lay delegates of the Evangelical Lutheran Congregations of Maryland and Virginia assembled in Grace Church at Winchester to organize their Synod. Pastor Kurtz was elected its first president. He occupied that high office for four consecutive terms and for thirty-two more years continued to be a member and advisor, always being considered "The Patriarch of the Synod."

In the same year, the General Synod became a reality at a conference in Hagerstown. This first national body of the Lutherans in America also chose the Pastor of Zion Church as its first president and twice thereafter re-elected him. Thus his untiring work was crowned. Suddenly Zion, once a little charge which had to plead hard for the occasional services of itinerant ministers in order to hear the Word of God, had a pulpit and a parsonage of national significance. Zion had reached its zenith. It had become the Mother Church of the Maryland Synod, and the quiet, pious Doctor of Divinity in the Baltimore parsonage was the president of the national body which at that time united nearly 45,000 Lutherans on the American continent.

While Pastor J. Daniel Kurtz was leading Zion to the height of its importance, the congregation was shaken by disturbances caused by the language issue. Every church founded by immigrants from non-English-speaking countries sooner or later in its history has been confronted with the problem of introducing the English language without denying the use of the old tongue to the services for those members who have not yet, or will never, acquire a command of the English language. If the German Lutheran congregation had heeded the far-sighted advice of its elders, Charles Wiesenthal and George Lindenberger, who as early as 1771, had advocated the tolerance of the English language, at least for the coming generations, the language transition would have taken place through a slow process of evolution. The unique location of Zion, however, in one of the nation's largest immigration ports, contributed largely to the fact that German remained the only language of preaching and teaching at Zion for many generations, in fact, until the First World War. This exclusive use of the German language was bought at a high price—a price which seemed so high to many members of Zion Church in the first decades of the 19th century that a conflict ensued which finally ended only after a pitiful period of strife and the loss of many a faithful parishioner.

Already as early as 1800, the Church Council was approached by several members who urged that body to consider the introduction of the English language. The Council voted down the proposal, and it is recorded that a number of people "with sorrow in their hearts felt compelled to leave the congregation." As there was no other Lutheran church in Baltimore at that time, those who left Zion either had to join English churches of other denominations or, as was quite frequently the case in the years to come, turned away altogether from participation in religious activities. Zion's membership consisted largely of American-born children and grandchildren of immigrants. In cases where both parents were German-speaking, the children generally had a good command of the German language. Being an urban element, the members of Zion lived scattered throughout the city, and many mingled freely with their Anglo-American neighbors. Intermarriage with English-speaking partners became frequent, and the children of such marriages were most likely reared in the English language. Consequently, Zion Church had an ever increasing number of members who either could not understand the German services at all or did so only with great difficulty.

Pastor Kurtz was much concerned about this development. Although American-born, he had been brought up in the solidly German regions of Pennsylvania, and he hoped that he could preserve Zion as a truly German Lutheran Church. In his "Historic Account of the Origin and the Growth of the Lutheran Congregation in Baltimore" written for the *Evangelisches Magazin* in 1813, he hinted at the difficulties which had been disturbing the harmony of his flock:

"A passion for innovation and the love for the English language caused the disruption in the congregation during the recent years. Yet, praised be God, the Church still flourishes and will probably remain a German congregation for a long time to come."

He seemed to be aware that the issue could no longer be evaded. His manifold duties did not leave him any time to envisage English services conducted by himself. In order to accommodate those members who could not understand German, he asked his nephew, the Rev. Benjamin Kurtz, to become his assistant at Zion. The young clergyman, who was perfectly bilingual, advocated English preaching for the sake of maintaining the ranks of Lutheranism. He left, however, a few months afterwards to accept a call in Hagerstown. His departure meant that again there were no services at Zion in the predominant language of the country.

In May 1816, a renewed request was submitted to the Church Council by the members favoring the English language. As no action ensued, a petition was circulated in the summer of the same year, signed by all those who opposed the continuation of monolingual services. The Church Council remained silent. After several weeks of waiting, an extraordinary meeting was called, which delegated Philip Uhler, Friedrich Leypold, Philip Endler, Daniel Hoffmann and Wilhelm Warner to incorporate the argument in favor of the introduction of English in a printed pamphlet, which was distributed to all members of the congregation. This pamphlet revealed the deep interest of those members in their church, which they had helped to build less than a decade before: "Look only at the number of young adults who have never been confirmed in our church, let alone in any other Christian church because they do not sufficiently understand the language. Shall we, as descendants of Lutheran parents, give up our faith, disavow their teachings after many of them came to this continent to enjoy this very faith free from fear and coercion? Shall we become Episcopalians, Presbyterians, Methodists?" The authors of the pamphlet went on to offer to let those who opposed the English language decide which part of the Sundays should be reserved for the English preaching. They even went so far as to pledge their continued financial support of the German services after they should have found an English Lutheran co-pastor, whom they would pay out of their own pockets, in order to avert a final split of the congregation. Touching and heart-rending was their final word: "If we should not succeed, we shall be forced to leave the congregation against our will, for the sake of the bread and water of life for our children. Your children and children's children will follow us."

This time a reply came. Conrad Schultz, Johann C. Steinbeck, Philip B. Sadtler, Friedrich Amelung, August Hammer, Friedrich Hammer and Johann Friedrich Friese protested on behalf of an alleged "five-sixths of the membership" against any further attempt at introducing the English language, and demanded that anyone thinking it indispensable to give his children English instructions in the Lutheran doctrines and to have English sermons for himself should leave the congregation. This was a clear answer. Pastor Kurtz was not referred to by either of the opposing factions.

The open outbreak of the language quarrel was not the only trial which Zion Church suffered during this period. By a tragic repetition of history, Zion was to witness once more the conflict of the young with the old which had darkened the first years of Pastor Kurtz's ministry. After the brief co-pastorate of Benjamin Kurtz in 1815, the whole burden of the pastoral work was back on Dr. Kurtz's shoulders. There was general agreement that a second pastor should be engaged. The question was, however, whether he was to be English- or German-speaking. After the final rebuttal of the English faction, only a second German pastor could be considered.

In 1822, during a temporary absence of Pastor Kurtz, whose synodical activities required much of his attention, a young and attractive German clergyman preached several sermons. The congregation was very much impressed by the Rev. Johann Uhlhorn, who had arrived from Germany a short while before, where he had been assistant pastor of the Lutheran church in Mannheim. The suggestion to offer him the co-pastorate at Zion found general approval. A memorandum signed by many members and "even those who were not members" was submitted to the Church Council. The Council conferred with Pastor Kurtz, who gladly consented to serve the congregation together with Pastor Johann Uhlhorn. The Council voted on this matter but could muster only a majority in favor of calling Pastor Uhlhorn, and not the two-thirds which the constitution required. Despite this short vote, on December 16, 1822, a formal invitation was extended to the Rev. Uhlhorn, which he accepted subsequently.

This was the final signal for the English faction of Zion's congregation. Their vote against engaging the German co-pastor, led by John Reese in the Church Council, had been completely ignored. Despite the continual neglect of their wishes by the majority, they had remained in the communion of Zion, hoping for an eventual change of mind on the part of their brethren. Now, the time had come when even the most faithful among them despaired, and together with John Reese several families of long standing left their old church. In October 1823, John Reese met with seven other former members of Zion to found the first English Lutheran congregation in Baltimore. They approached the Synod of Maryland, built their own church, and in 1827 had their first regular pastor, the Rev. John Gottlieb Morris who wrote about the attitude of Zion: "Some of the influential members opposed us directly, but I had the satisfaction not many years after, of receiving some of these very men and their large families into my church." Pastor Kurtz did not put any obstacles in the way of the new English Lutheran congregation, hoping that it would contribute to a restoration of peace at Zion and at the same time prevent the anglicized Lutherans from losing their old faith.

But the minds of the people at Zion were so much stirred up by the recent conflicts that soon the new co-pastor, whether or not he wished it, was drawn into the vortices of a violent congregational battle. The young, cultured and talented man was such an excellent preacher that he soon outshone old Pastor Kurtz. He was certainly not a person to engage in intrigues and arguments, but soon he had a following among a large segment of the congregation; whereas many others proved their allegiance to the old pastor by violently opposing the new one. Things finally went so far that two councils were elected in 1829, in a tumultuous double ballot. New elections were held in the same year and in the first half of 1830, but these resulted only in an increased confusion. In the church archives is preserved a vivid description of a Sunday morning service during which the warring parties broke up the worship and carried out their deplorable quarrels in front of the altar.

In order to bring about a reconciliation, to restore the peace and unity of the congregation, about which both pastors were profoundly concerned, a memorandum was submitted to all members on June 1, 1830, analyzing the causes of the disturbances, examining the position of the Church Council and the lawful procedure of the election of council members in accordance with the constitution.

As Pastor Uhlhorn felt that his presence at Zion had against his will led to the disruption, he wanted to prevent the break-up of the venerable church. He was determined, out of his respect for his elder colleague, to leave Zion rather than to see Pastor Kurtz forced out of his position. He submitted his resignation. On July 29, 1830, the combined Church Council met under the chairman, Philip Muth, and refused this sudden resignation.

Under the guidance of both pastors, the congregation was finally united again. One Council was elected on August 24, 1830, and a new constitution was adopted.

At the same time a new "Plan of Incorporation of Zion Church of the City of Baltimore," was adopted, based on the constitution and in pursuance of the Act of 1802, which had superseded previous regulations under which Zion Church was incorporated for the first time in 1800.

The new constitution defined clearly the confessional character of the church, the language used for the services, the competence of the two pastors and the Church Council.

The first section stated expressly:

> "The presently engaged preachers and their duly elected successors shall at regular times on Sundays and holidays, at funerals and other solemnities publicly, implicitly, and edifyingly announce the Word of God according to the apostles and prophets, and the unaltered Augsburg Confession."

The divine services should forever be conducted in the German language, and, as Article 1 provided expressly, "this clause of agreement according to which the preaching in English is prohibited shall never be subject to change." The Church Council should henceforth consist of eight elders, four deacons and the pastor. In the case of the church's having more than one pastor, the elder pastor alone should belong to the Church Council. At the same time, all Council members were designated as the trustees of the church's property. The constitution was signed by President Dr. J. Daniel Kurtz, by Peter Sauerwein, Carl Bohn, Philip Muth, Christian Capito, Christoph von Hollen, Johann Super, Carsten Torney and Carl W. Karthaus as elders, Gottlieb J. Medinger, George Sauerwein, Friedrich Kummer and Johann J. Medinger as deacons.

For almost three years after the restoration of peace the two pastors worked side by side, alternating the services. But Pastor Kurtz soon felt that the labors and the quarrels had taken his old vigor from him and the years had eaten his strength. Much of his energy, which could have been employed toward a further build-up of his church both locally and in the Synods which he served, had been wasted by the unfortunate dissensions of his flock. The brilliant young man who stood in Zion's pulpit every other Sunday seemed to mean more to the congregation. Pastor Kurtz represented the old school; whereas the youth of the congregation felt attracted by the sermons of Uhlhorn, who had a grasp of the new times. It is recorded:

"Upon reaching his seventieth year of age, Dr. Daniel Kurtz submitted his resignation in 1832. The Church Council accepted it at once. The grateful congregation who owed him so much, but who had also filled his last years at Zion with deep sorrow voted him a considerable annuity and the use of the parsonage for the rest of his life. For the last time he stepped up to the pulpit and preached a valedictory from the words, 'Finally brethren, farewell. Be perfect, be of good comfort, be of one mind, live in peace; and the God of love and peace shall be with you.'"

When Pastor Kurtz finished his last sermon, he had completed a pastorate of forty-seven years. He left the scene of his lifelong work with the hope that a youthful minister would continue to rebuild the congregation on the firm foundations that he had laid.

He had built the church in which, in 1955, a grateful posterity will celebrate the 200th anniversary of the founding of the congregation. He had led the Lutherans of Baltimore out of the isolation of the pioneer days into the center of the church-at-large. The Maryland Synod, which he helped to found and which he led in its first crucial years, has outlasted many other church organizations and is today, more than ever before, the rallying point and the focus of Lutheranism. His name is forever connected with the General Synod of the Evangelical Lutheran Church in America. Already during his lifetime he was considered the patriarch of the church. For Zion, however, he was the greatest, although not the most spectacular, leader who ever occupied its pulpit. As the following chapter will indicate, the people of Zion were scattered, but wherever they went, they remained true to the faith of their fathers. Zion became the salt of many Lutheran churches that sprang up in Baltimore. After his resignation, Dr. Kurtz also remained faithful to his former parishioners. Often he was called upon to preach and to perform the rites of the church. When he was ninety years old, he officiated at the exercises connected with the laying of the cornerstone of two new Lutheran Churches in Baltimore, both founded by former members of Zion.

In the ninety-second year of his age, he conducted the funeral of one of his former parishioners. A church paper thus described the occasion: "He delivered an impressive address in German, which would have reflected credit on his head and heart, even in the prime of his life. The scene was exquisitely touching: there, in the center of the parlor, stood the time-worn veteran, who had endured the peltings, and passed through the vicissitudes of nearly one century, surrounded by the grand-children and great grand-children of his primitive contemporaries. Supported by one hand resting on the back of a chair, and by the other on his faithful cane, he stood erect, and bore glorious testimony to the doctrine of salvation by faith in a crucified Redeemer."

Thus, his entire life had been directed by faith. This testimony of his last year in life completes a circle of harmony which underlay all his actions. "I am not one of those who, through storms and earthquakes, have been brought to a knowledge of the Savior, but through the still small voice of the precedent and preparing grace of God" he wrote in his autobiography. Amidst the mountains of work that he overcame and the tempests of strife that accompanied the last years of his pastorate, he calmly and determinedly went forward in the faithful discharge of his duties. There was a beautiful harmony in his life and actions. Everywhere he inspired confidence and love. His example produced a decided impression on the minds of those who came within the circle of his influence.

In the face of God, he was meek, in the face of man, he took a determined stand. There was no wavering from the religious views under whose influence he had been reared, and yet, he was exceedingly tolerant to those who were of different persuasions. He freely associated with clergymen of other denominations and brought about a fruitful cooperation among the churches of Baltimore. He was one of the founders of the Maryland Bible Society, and was active in many other religious and civic organizations, time and again bringing Zion Church into the work for the general welfare of the community.

Despite the conflicts which involved his congregation, the Rev. John G. Morris wrote this tribute to the patriarch of the Maryland Synod: "He was the most blameless man I ever knew. He had encountered some troublesome spirits in his church, but in all that time not the slightest whisper of wrong doing on his part was ever heard, and he went down to his grave with a name untarnished as the whitest snow."

On June 30, 1856, Pastor Kurtz died, ninety-three years old. Lutherans and non-Lutherans from all over the state and from many distant places laid him to rest in the Greenmount Cemetery. Upon his death the Maryland Synod recorded in a memorial statement: "As a preacher he was ardent, impressive, and thorough-scriptural. As a pastor he was faithful, self-denying, and exemplary. As a Christian he was conscientious, humble, and sincere. In every relation of life his example was worthy of imitation."

If statistics alone could express the balance of a great life, Daniel Kurtz was one of the most diligent servants of the church: During his ministry he baptized 5156 persons, buried 2521, and solemnized 2386 marriages. For Zion this simple, great and uncompromising man, however, marked out the path to which the congregation was to return almost one hundred years after his death, a tribute to his life and work which is more potent than all eulogies and evaluations written during the past.

With Pastor Kurtz's resignation in 1832, the first distinct phase in the history of Zion Church came to on end. Up to this time, the Baltimore congregation had undergone the same ups and downs, the same conflicts and upheavals which we find in the histories of other Lutheran congregations. The presence of strong characters among the leadership, such as John Siegfried Gerock and J. Daniel Kurtz among the pastors, Charles Wiesenthal and Moritz Wörschler among the laymen, contributed an extraordinary accent to the events which had shaken the congregation. The last major issue, the language question, although unnecessarily dragged along for several decades, and finally disposed of in a rather inglorious manner, was also common to all other Lutheran churches in America. All of them, at one time or another, faced the painful necessity of accommodation to the language of the land. For Zion this problem was now solved. The English-speaking members had been forced out of the communion, and as the result of this clear separation the church could now develop as a German-Lutheran church.

We have traced the history of Zion Church from the early beginnings to its zenith, when Zion's pastor was the president of the General Synod and of the regional synod. It was a clear, straight road upwards. After the first loss of substance due to the language issue, the membership still remained very strong in numbers, and the common attachment to the use of the German tongue in worship and teaching could only serve as an additional moment of strength. Thus, the language issue alone could not be the cause for the deep rift that divided the congregation, nor could it be personal loyalty to the old spiritual guide on the one hand, and to the young, attractive clergyman on the other hand, those two who for ten years had worked, at times side by side and at other times on opposite sides, but always serving the same congregation.

Daniel Kurtz refrained from any judgment upon the events at Zion after he had retired, and thus left without any word that could have thrown light on the actions of the Church Council and its position with regard to the confessional premises of the church. The Rev. Johann Uhlhorn, who was now the sole spiritual leader, had a considerable following among the congregation after his ten years as co-pastor. To win the other part of the congregation was his immediate task before he could even consider any other undertaking. He had received an excellent ministerial education in Germany, which qualified him eminently to revive the church and reconcile the old-school, conservative members with his modern, progressive thought, without impairing the fundamental character of the faith. At the outset of his pastorate he had the advantage of being fully familiar with the problems and needs of Zion. Ten years as co-pastor was an unusual preparation for his work.

Born in Bremen in 1794, an illegitimate child, he was reared in extremely poor circumstances. Nevertheless, through the sacrifices of his mother and the aid of the church, he prepared for a career as a teacher. As a young lad he was *Unterlehrer* at the *Deutsche Domschule* in Bremen, and studied classical subjects in the *Latei-*

nische Domschule, where he enrolled in April 1808. He decided to become a preacher instead of a teacher and turned toward the study of theology. In 1812 he entered the University of Strassburg in Alsace. After the end of the war with Napoleon, he served for several years as an assistant of the pastor at the Lutheran parish in Mannheim in the Palatinate.

When he first came to this country, he was described as a rather polished, fashionable ecclesiastic, whose appearance caused concern to many old timers at Zion. He wore rings in his ears, and in his attire were other evidences of more expensive and scrupulous attention to his person than was common among clergymen in the American Lutheran churches. His gradual adjustment to the simpler customs of American life was gratefully acknowledged by his friends and his opponents at Zion. He was admired for his remarkable knowledge, and many exuberant tales are recorded of his preaching ability and his familiarity with classic culture. His delicate nature was likened to that of Melanchthon. In all respects he seemed to be the right man for Zion Church.

Before effecting any plans of his own, he desired to visit briefly his native Bremen. The Church Council granted him a leave in 1833. On March 22, 1834, he died from a sudden illness, soon after his arrival in his old home. Zion was left a flock without a shepherd. Now it became evident that during all the bickering over formalities, the unfortunate eruptions of pride, the malcontent and discord of a few, the spiritual needs of the people had been slighted. The congregation had lingered along from Sunday to Sunday, but the emphasis on their confession of faith had been neglected under the impact of other problems. "A down-trodden congregation, split into parties, upset by ugly obsessions, a band of people who called themselves Christian, but who lacked the first prerogatives of Christianity, love and peace" was the impression of a contemporary upon a first contact with the people of Zion.

Pastor Wilhelm Domeier, whom the Church Council had engaged during the absence of the Rev. Uhlhorn, did nothing to improve the situation. As a successor to the man who had died so unexpectedly, he was highly unsuitable. Charged with repeated and excessive drunkenness, he was sent on his way. For many Sundays the pulpit of Zion remained empty. The Church Council alone bore the responsibilities of continuing the existence of the congregation. It assumed a position of absolute rule, seemingly with little authorization from a large segment of the congregation.

A new pastor was finally found, the Rev. John Peter Haesbert. Now something became evident that so far had never come into the open: the confessional foundation of Zion Church was shaky. Pastor Haesbert, an unusually orthodox minister, began violently to rebuke the Church Council for its lax attitude toward the doctrines of the church. Without regard and understanding for the position which the Church Council of Zion had acquired traditionally, he attempted to swing the church over into orthodoxy. He encountered an opposition which was just as violent as his own actions. For the reasons that his own character was not without reproach and that it was "a disgusting fight which he led against the church council," he was dismissed. Now an unexepected, tragical episode occurred in that about 150 members announced their resignation from membership in Zion Church. After some hesitation, Pastor Haesbert organized a new congregation to gather together all these former members of Zion. On November 1, 1835, the "Second German Evangelical Lutheran Church of the Unaltered Augsburg Confession" came into being and bought a vacant brick church building on the corner of Holliday and Saratoga Streets. The words "Augsburg Confession" were inscribed in large, ostentatious letters on the building. Again members of Zion provided the membership for a new Lutheran church in Baltimore. Pastor Haesbert, the leader of this spectacular exodus, otherwise a humble, upright and honest man, became involved in family difficulties which caused his removal to New Orleans. After a short pastorate there, he left for Brazil where he became a prominent Lutheran organizer whose memory is still today held in high esteem. Pastor Daniel Kurtz, though 81 years old, stood by his former parishioners from Zion and preached to them until March 1845, when he installed the Rev. F. C. Wyneken as the pastor of the Second German Lutheran Church.

But there was still Zion Church. There was an altar without a servant, a pulpit without a preacher. The cantor and the regular schoolteacher had also left. The loss of a large percentage of the membership raised the question whether Zion would continue to exist. The communion records in the church register end in 1833. No hand had made any entries since that year. The school, for which the Church Council once had far-reaching plans, was without a regular teacher. Here is a description of what it looked like in September 1835: "In the unclean, desolate school-room whose floor was unswept and whose walls and windows were festooned with spiderwebs, I found seventeen unhappy children of various ages and both sexes ranged on shaky benches around a long broken-down table. Physical and mental poverty cried loud to me from all sides." Only the two graveyards of the church, one at the eastern and one at the western end of the city, saw regular activity. The number of burials remained similar to that of the by-gone days. Baptisms, marriages and the number of confirmands were lower than at any time in the past half-century. Despair had taken the place of hope.

The old Zion was doomed. There was little left of the Zion that three generations had built with their labors and their sacrifices. It calls back to our minds the days when the neighbor on the hill dug away the sand on which the humble little church house of the Lutherans stood. Strife and hatred now had broken away the firm foundation on which the congregation of Zion had rested. A new builder had to come, or the year 1835 would have been the sad end of an eighty-year history of Zion Church.

CHAPTER THREE

Scheib's Church
1835-1896

THE NEW BUILDER came in September 1835. Here, we must leave the sources which so far have given us the information on the German Lutheran congregation in Baltimore. The last loose leaves of the *Kirchen-Archiv,* which have so faithfully guided us through the first eighty years of Zion's history, end here. The reports of the annual conventions of the synods no longer bear witness to the developments which were to take place in Zion Church. Only once, much later, we find a reference in the Lutheran Cyclopedia: "The mother church was alienated from the Lutheran Church and from synodical connections through a rationalist pastor."

A member of the consistory of Zion Church, while visiting New York in the summer of 1835, attended a service in St. Matthew's Lutheran Church and heard the sermon of the young assistant to the venerable, old pastor, Frederick William Geissenhainer. Upon inquiry, Dr. Geissenhainer informed the visitor from Baltimore that his assistant, Henry Scheib, had just come to New York from Germany in April and as he was without a charge, had been taken in by him until some congregation would call him. Zion Church, or better the skeleton of the old congregation which remained after the cleavage of 1823 and the mass exodus of 1834-35, did not hesitate for long to call the Rev. Scheib to deliver several sermons at Zion.

One month after his coming to Baltimore, on October 18, 1835, the Church Council elected Scheib as the regular pastor of Zion Church. His sermons had met with the approval of a majority, and besides, the church could no longer wait for a permanent minister, lest it dissolve completely. There were still a few members of the old conservative stock who had not left when Pastor Haesbert drew a large segment of Zion's congregation into the whirlpool of a confessional battle. Most members, however, who had remained were recent immigrants from Europe. They had gone through the many decades of war. They had been exposed to the liberal ideas that had spread over Europe after the French Revolution. For them, orthodoxy as Pastor Haesbert represented it, and pietistic conservativism as Pastor Kurtz had preached it, were utterly alien. They sought a church that would provide something to hold on to in the tribulations of the immigrant's life, until the final adjustment. They expected a church that would open its doors on Sunday morning, that would instruct their children and, apart from edifying its members during the services and requiring the usual contribution, would leave them alone. They were generally better educated than the pioneers of the 18th century, and elaborate, sophisticated sermons such as Pastor Uhlhorn had provided corresponded more to their taste than did the gospel ministry of Father Kurtz, who could only promise them "For five decades I have preached the same unchangeable Gospel of salvation by faith in Jesus, and I have nothing else to present to you today."

They chose Henry Scheib. Twenty-seven years old when he first occupied the pulpit of Zion, he had been reared in the very same environment as many of Zion's new members. He was born on July 8, 1808, in Bacharach, a small town on the Rhine. His father was a vintner in modest circumstances, but was determined to give Henry, the oldest of five children, the best available education. A parish school of the Reformed Church, where he received his elementary training, evoked a negative reaction in the young pupil. In his autobiography he wrote: "These instructions under an old, outmoded school tyrant and later catechumen lessons under a minister who knew more about horse-trading than about theology were unimaginably miserable and utterly fruitless." This first encounter with the Reformed Church school was never forgotten by Scheib, and in his earliest years a spirit of rebellion developed within him that could neither be tamed by the strict *Latein-Schule* where his father sent him when he was ten years old to acquire the knowledge of classical languages and natural sciences, nor by the *Humanistische Gymnasium* in Kreuznach, where he prepared for university studies.

HEINRICH SCHEIB
1835-1896

From his own notes on his early life we can discern his critical approach to all learning and studying as it was offered by the institutions that he attended. Natural sciences, geometry, history and geography with their actual and factual content were the subjects in which he found delight and satisfaction in penetrating to the facts, the truth behind all that he read and listened to. With the same sincere desire to arrive at the truth, he turned to the Holy Scriptures after he had decided to study theology. The newly founded University of Bonn admitted him as a student to the Theological Faculty. His mastery of Hebrew, Greek, and Latin enabled him to read both Testaments and the writing of the church fathers in the original.

He related in his autobiography how the principal of the Gymnasium in Kreuznach read the New Testament with his students in the original Greek and approached the text by using other critical methods than were employed in regard to temporal writings. Scheib rebelled at once when his teacher time and again warned of false interpretations of the Scriptures and attempted to prove with "hair-raising exegetical tricks" that the New Testament could only be interpreted in full agreement with the doctrines taught by the church.

Then Henry Scheib decided that the truth of the Gospel could only be arrived at through the same modern, scientific methods of critical reading that were commonly employed in the study of all classical texts and even of the Old Testament. This conviction formed the basis of his liberalism, or, as his opponents later called them, "his rationalist views." His university curriculum at Bonn included pedagogy, medicine, natural sciences and languages. Upon completion of his studies, he found that he could not be placed in a parish immediately, for want of an opening. Actually, however, the ecclesiastical authorities had become aware of his liberal attitudes and his disregard for the doctrinal stand of the church.

A scholarship at the University of Utrecht opened to him new opportunities to satisfy his boundless hunger for learning. At the ancient Dutch school of theology, where all lectures were delivered in Latin, Scheib deepened his knowledge of the literature of the Bible and of the Reformation; at the same time, however, the immovable dogmatism as it was taught in Utrecht in the spirit of the Dortrecht Articles of Faith increased his opposition to anything that he could not acquire through his own rationalizing method of investigation.

In the summer of 1834, before he concluded his studies at Utrecht, he visited Germany. His native Rhineland, for two decades under Prussian rule, was not at all hospitable to him. If we can rely on his own version of this visit, he was brought to trial for his liberal views and was informed that despite his ministerial training he would have to serve a three-year tour of duty with the Prussian army. Outside of Prussia, the German states were under the reactionary influence of Metternich, and a liberal of the cloth was nowhere looked upon with favor. Henry Scheib decided to embark for America. He left from Rotterdam in December 1834, and reached New York in April 1835.

In the New World he did not meet with a hearty welcome. Often, in his later years, he related how forsaken he felt in the strange land, and how he stood in the streets of New York like a wanderer lost in a vast forest. In the person of the venerable senior of the Lutheran clergy of New York, Dr. Geissenhainer, he finally found a friend who granted him the use of his pulpit, some time before the call to Baltimore reached him.

The congregation which Pastor Scheib began to serve in 1835, "down-trodden, upset by ugly obsessions" as it was described before, received him with much good will. But the cleavage which had been left so wide open and all the mutual distrust that divided the flock remained. With his great energy and his uncompromising faith in the victory of truth over ignorance, of light as he saw it over the darkness, the young pastor made a healthy start toward better relations within the congregation. "To win them for the better seemed hopeless enough at the beginning. But surrounded by theological accusers and blackmailers, under blame and shame, so low and loveless, he sowed the seed of peace, of love, of education and of morality; what he had to tell his congregation, he demonstrated in his own blameless life," his consistory testified for him when he was called to defend his beliefs and his actions.

The sermons he preached from the pulpit of Zion were something new. These people had to be lifted up again to hope and love and neighborliness. He put before them the man Jesus Christ, who loved, and helped and admonished. He gave them the example of the woman Mary, who brought up her child Jesus to believe in the good, the beautiful, and the true. He called on the people to think for themselves while reading the Bible. He baptized and confirmed, married young couples and buried the dead, truly only a few, as his flock was small; but every Sunday new hearers came, some to shake their heads in bewilderment, others to stay and join Zion Church.

Almost four years went by, and on April 14, 1839, Pastor Scheib stood up for re-election by the congregation. There had been some grumbling and some warnings from older members who could not accept what the new pastor preached. It was so different from anything which they had heard before. They respected his personality and the fine work of reuniting the congregation that he had done, but conscience would not let them rest. Why did old Pastor Kurtz, who was still occupying the parsonage, no longer attend the service? Why, on Sunday morning, did he go to the English Lutheran Church to listen to English services instead of the German preached at Zion, the language to which he had clung to the last? They began to question the things they heard from the mouth of the pastor, and finally on the eve of his proposed re-election they wrote a pamphlet which was circulated among all members of Zion Church.

Some who read this circular urging the congregation not to re-elect Pastor Scheib were stunned; many filled with anger. How could anyone so openly denounce the young and forceful pastor who had devoted all his days and many of his night hours to bring the church back to life and restore the congregational peace? Why was this upright man suddenly accused by members of his own church who had silently attended his services for four years? The circular went around from hand to hand: "Our beloved Zion Church is known to be a Lutheran Church. Our church was built by Lutherans to be and to remain a Lutheran Church where the sacred truths of the Gospel in accordance with the Lutheran Catechism and the Augsburg Confession shall be preached"—nobody had ever questioned this. All members considered themselves Lutherans, and never had they heard their pastor denounce the Augsburg Confession or the Catechism of Martin Luther. Were not his sermons full of references to the great reformer and leader Martin Luther? But the pamphlet went on to accuse Pastor Scheib:

"We claim that the Rev. Scheib, who is the candidate for the pastorate of our Zion Church, is by no means a true Evangelical Lutheran preacher, but in his beliefs approaches heresy and therefore he cannot be re-elected in accordance with our constitution. For our constitution requires that our minister be not a Unitarian or Universalist but a pious, faithful, decided Lutheran, which the Rev. Scheib is not, as we think is quite evident."

How could anyone dare to pronounce such judgment on the man whose kindness and frankness had won him the respect and love of so many among his members? Here were people of the same Zion Church imploring their brethren to send their young pastor away: "Would it not be infinitely better if our church remained empty, and our children were left without religious instructions instead of helping to propagate these false, un-Biblical, soul-murdering doctrines? Would you not rather abjure the Lutheran church, abandon our beautiful house of God to the Unitarians, and declare yourself publicly against the Lutheran catechism, the Augsburg confession, and the divine teachings of the Gospel?"

This pamphlet was not signed by anyone. Its anonymous character contributed much to the violent rebuttal which it provoked from the large majority of the congregation. Immediately after it was circulated, the vestry and the directorium of Zion School convened, and on the following day the reply, endorsed by 175 members with their signatures, was given to the printer and soon afterwards distributed to all members of the church who could be reached.

Under the date of April 10, 1839, the vestry under its president, Conrad Lindemann, consisting of Johann Berger, D. H. Allers, Otto Torney, Henry Huber, W. Meusel, and G. H. Wetter, and Carsten Torney, president of Zion School directorium, Dr. A. Wegner, C. Simon, G. H. Mittnacht, and Gottlieb Medinger, members of the directorium, adopted the resolution which was embodied in the reply to the anonymous charges: "We consider that pamphlet as an attempt of ill-willed people who intend to spread unrest and discord among a peaceful congregation. First of all because the authors of this libelous writ have not the courage to mention their names, and secondly because an honest man who might not have been content with the teachings of Pastor Scheib should have stood up against them a long time ago." Rebuking the various charges of the accusers, the reply went on: "Resolved, that the vestry considers it its duty to declare publicly:

> 1.) that Pastor Scheib has always endeavored by his preachings to spread the conscientiousness of virtue and true Christ-love according to the Augsburg Confession among his listeners. He has just as vigorously presented vice and sin in its infamy. 2.) that he always supported these teachings by his own blameless example. He has not only most faithfully tended to his office as preacher but also has proved by his manifold acts of charity that he is not a hireling in the vineyard of the Lord. Furthermore has the church council the great pleasure to state that the public and private character of Pastor Scheib is above any reproach."

Four days later the congregation assembled to vote on the motion to re-elect Pastor Scheib for the next four years. With 254 against 38 votes, his ministry was approved by the vast majority of Zion's congregation.

We have read in the preceding chapters what an eminent part Zion's pastor, Dr. Daniel Kurtz, played in the synodical organization of the Lutheran Church. Gradually the synods developed from mere ministerial associations into the centralizing bodies of Lutheran endeavors. Not only pastors but also representatives from the congregations attended the annual conventions. What was originally only a pastoral membership became a congregational membership. In this development Zion Church had no part.

When Scheib began his work as an assistant at St. Matthew's Church in New York City he was accepted by the New York Ministerium. After his coming to Baltimore, he retained his membership with this synodical body in New York. After he was reinstated for an additional period of four years as the pastor of Zion Church, in April 1839, he decided to declare his resignation from membership in the New York Ministerium "out of a sense of duty, as the considerable distance and the expenses connected with the journey would not permit him to attend the required annual meetings of the synod."

This resignation was refused by the Ministerium. Meanwhile a letter signed by seven members of Zion Church, Philip B. Sadler, John C. Rau, John M. Mühlhofer, A. Hildebrandt, Frederick

Kummer, John Mayer, and Peter Sauerwein had reached the New York Synod. Under the date of September 10, 1839, these members, most of them of long standing and many of them former vestrymen, wrote: "We have reason to believe that the Rev. Scheib does not preach the word of God in accordance with our Evangelical Lutheran Confession of Faith." They also stated that many members, especially from among the old membership and their sons, had left Zion Church on account of Scheib's teachings and that others contemplated following them unless "the unaltered Evangelical-Lutheran doctrine should become dominant again in our church. It is hard, really hard for the old members who contributed to the erection of their beautiful Zion Church. They gave voluntarily and cheerfully, expecting that their church would remain for themselves and their descendants what it was built for. Now in the face of a religious instruction that is alien to them, they are forced to leave their church. Oh, it is hard."

On September 23, 1839, a prompt reply came from the Rev. Philip H. Mayer on behalf of the Ministerium. As the accusations were one-sided, though very grave, the Ministerium forwarded a copy of this plea to Pastor Scheib with the request that he present himself to a committee of investigation to answer the charges brought against him with regard to his preaching and conducting the instruction in Zion School. Scheib was willing to appear before this committee provided it could prove that it had a right to refuse his previous resignation. The Church Council, however, was so indignant at this interference by the Ministerium that they wrote immediately to the committee which was to have investigated the activities of Pastor Scheib. The letter was written in sharp, unmistakable terms: "It is the express desire of the Church Council that Pastor Scheib shall not follow the demand to appear, as the Church Council will not concede the right to any Synod to interfere with the affairs of Zion Church, which has always been independent and will remain so. According to the constitution of Zion Church, nobody had a right to demand justification from the preacher in matters of the church without having informed the Church Council or upon the request of the Church Council, and neither of these requirements had been fulfilled."

The New York Ministerium never answered this letter of the vestry of Zion Church. Instead *The Lutheran Observer,* a church paper edited in Baltimore, several weeks later published a resolution of the New York Ministerium to the effect that Pastor Scheib was "stricken from the roll of the Ministerium." This publication caused Zion's Church Council to issue a lengthy statement reiterating the various events that had led to severing the relations between the pastor of Zion Church and the New York Ministerium. Among all these polemics stand the words regarding Pastor Scheib's personal conduct, which formed a part of the resolution issued by the Ministerium: "Not a whisper was breathed against your moral conduct, and testimony was borne to much that is highly laudable in your deportment and life." This testimony was the most encouraging and reassuring factor of the entire controversy for Pastor Scheib. The Church Council stood by him firmly and he felt responsible to his own Council alone, for his work as the minister of Zion Church.

The Maryland Synod did not interfere at all. It watched the happenings closely, and from the fact that the resolutions of the New York Ministerium were published in *The Lutheran Observer,* which was edited by the Rev. Benjamin Kurtz, who under his uncle, J. Daniel Kurtz, once had been an assistant pastor of Zion Church, we can infer that its attitude coincided with that of the New York sister synod.

Thus, from 1839 on Zion Church belonged to that class of religious bodies which is characterized in ecclesiastical language as "having adopted the 'Independent' or 'Congregational' form of church government without being subject to the jurisdiction or control of any synod composed of delegates from different associated churches." Zion Church had become Scheib's Church.

Rejected by the Lutheran ecclesiastical authorities and desiring to stand alone, Zion's flock and its lone shepherd were not spared further tribulations.

In the spring of 1837 a flash flood had swept over the premises of the church, severely damaging the school house and the parsonage and also impairing the foundations of the church itself. The school, of which we shall speak in a separate chapter, was repaired at once, and subsequently enlarged. Not so the parsonage. It was still occupied by the old pastor, J. Daniel Kurtz, to whom the use of the parsonage had been granted for his lifetime by the congregation when he retired in 1832. On June 14, 1837, Pastor Kurtz wrote a letter to Philip B. Sadler, one of the few old Zion members who still belonged to the church. We could have omitted this letter in our history of Zion Church, but it is such a disheartening document of ingratitude toward a man who represented a world which the new people at Zion thought they had left behind, that we have included it. As so often occurs when new times have dawned those who have done their duty in the past are forgotten and neglected.

For the last time we read the handwriting of Daniel Kurtz, so familiar to us from his many careful entries in the church records: "I take the liberty to inform you that the parsonage which I occupy has suffered considerable damage during the flood, which will greatly impair my living quarters if repairs are not made immediately. The soil is partly swept away, down to the foundation of the building, the pavement is torn open, and the stone steps leading up to the entrance of the house are completely undermined and are about to tumble altogether if no attempts are made at repairing them. I hope that it is not expected of me that I have the repairs made at my own expense, as the losses I have suffered through the destruction of everything that was in the basement are very great, and besides I have to repair my apartment. Please give this request your consideration and if necessary inform the Church Council of it."

As no reply came nor any action was taken, the old minister quietly packed up his belongings and moved uptown. He never said nor wrote any word of complaint. Once, when a friend asked him about the humiliations he had suffered at the hands of the church in the service of which he had spent his life, he remarked: "We will say nothing about these. I have long since forgiven all my enemies, and prayed God also to blot out their sins. They no doubt think they were right and intended not so much harm to me as might be supposed."

Three years later Philip B. Sadler and a group of some fifty older members of Zion also left the congregation. Some of their names are on the list of those whose contributions built the church in 1808. "The last troublemakers left in 1840," the Church Council observed later, and in the brief history of Zion Church published in 1905, we read: "The malcontents were to a large degree eliminated; the last of them left in 1840."

It seemed that of the old days, only the church building was left. Everything else was filled with a new spirit, and the determined will power and the eloquence of Pastor Scheib had created an atmosphere which left no room for the memories of former times.

But again the elements broke loose over Zion. An old, well-thumbed newspaper file gives us the eye-witness report: "At about half-past three o'clock on Monday morning, March 30, 1840, the inhabitants in the neighborhood of Gay Street were alarmed by the cry of fire. The flames at the time of the alarm were breaking through the roof and windows of the workshop in the rear of Edwin S. Tarr's cabinet warerooms on North Gay Street, next to the German Lutheran Church. In a short time the roof of the church caught fire from the intense heat, and the venerable edifice soon became a heap of ruins. Owing to a heavy fall of rain, which prevailed during the whole time the fire was raging, the fire did not extend."

While the ruins of the church were still smouldering, Pastor Scheib called upon the people of Zion to rebuild their house of worship without delay. As the outside walls had been spared, he decided upon a plan of reconstruction that would largely preserve the outward appearance of the old building. On November 8, 1840, the church was reopened with a dedication service under the motto "To Strive for Reason's Victory." The tower on the front, however, was not rebuilt. The inside was considerably changed. Pastor Scheib radically applied the Reformed concept of simplicity. Pulpit and altar, both painted white, were separated from the rest of the room by a simple iron railing. The walls and the ceiling were given a light grey coat, while all the woodwork was kept in a yellow shade of oak wood. The interior, in its box-like shape, reminded many a visitor of a Puritan house of worship. For Pastor Scheib and many of his parishioners, this expression of utmost simplicity fully coincided with their private lives outside of the church and was in complete harmony with their endeavor to approach religion with an open and critical mind, devoid of any ornaments and mystery.

On April 17, 1840, August Müller announced the formation of an association of Zion members to raise funds for a new organ. H. Knauf of Philadelphia built the instrument and it was installed in the same year. In 1843, a swell was added to the organ.

The church choir, *Singe Verein,* which had already participated in the dedication services of Zion Church in 1808, was given new impetus after Pastor Scheib came to Zion. Together with one of the teachers at Zion School, Friedrich Lüdeking, Scheib founded the first German singing society in Baltimore, the *Liederkranz* (and the second one in the United States, the *Philadelphia Männerchor,* founded in 1835, being the oldest), which held its first meeting on December 30, 1836, in the rooms of Zion Church. In the following year Philip M. Wolsieffer came to Baltimore, in response to an invitation by Scheib to be director of the *Liederkranz.* When the society presented Andreas Romberg's version of Schiller's "Song of the Bell" in 1840, during the rededication service of Zion Church, it created a scandal among the more conservative element, who were opposed to the inclusion of this extremely worldly poem in divine services. In the following years Pastor Scheib frequently called on the *Liederkranz* society to help him embellish his lecture-services.

Less than one decade after Pastor Scheib's arrival in Baltimore, Zion Church had undergone such a complete change that the new church can justly be considered a successor to the Old Zion rather than its continuation. The old membership, as we have seen, had turned away from Zion, and even the elements had contributed to bring into being a house of worship that very little resembled the Zion of 1808. At first Pastor Scheib and his vestry had attempted to conduct the affairs of the church according to the constitution of 1830, by interpreting its provisions in the light of the new events at Zion. More and more, however, this constitution proved to stand in the way of the many innovations. Several sections had been suspended by unanimous action of the congregation.

After several weeks of deliberations, the vestry met, in January 1844, and adopted a new constitution. The president of the vestry, D. H. Allers, and the secretary, Johann Brühl, wrote in the preface to the published edition of this constitution that it was merely a renewal of the 1830 constitution with "such alterations as have become necessary since." Upon closer investigation, however, we find that this document is a far cry from any constitution which Zion Church had had during the past.

Section 2, Article I defined the purpose of the congregation as follows: "The purpose of the church is the propagation of reasonable religiosity and genuine morality according to the principles of the Gospel." Possibly with the text of the original deeds in view, the term "Augsburg Confession" appears in Section 9, Article I. However, it is only a vague reference: "As the congregation of Zion, being a Protestant-Christian Church in accordance with the principles of the reformers, and the clear statement of the Augsburg Confession, Article 28 et alia, recognizes as standard and rule of faith and doctrine only the Gospel, the preacher has to annunciate only a Gospel according to Scriptures and reason. He must not preach doctrines which either are not contained in the New Testament or are in contradiction to it, after a reasonable and scientific text criticism."

After the preceding controversy with the New York Synod we can easily understand why this article (VII) was included in Section 9: "The preacher of this congregation shall not be a member of any religious association or a church society (Synod) which is based on principles contradicting Article I of this constitution." Despite these fundamental changes the name of the congregation was to remain "German Evangelical-Lutheran Zion Congregation in Baltimore." (Sec. 1, Art. I). The language was clearly defined in Section 1, Art. II: "As the church was founded *by* Germans and *for* Germans all *preaching* and all transactions *shall be conducted in the German language* as long as there are still five members who wish the German language for public worship."

The articles are quoted in full, since they have for many years, for almost a century, dominated the thinking at Zion Church. As time progressed, they were considered the "Zion tradition," a somewhat sacred heritage which subsequent generations, although no longer able to adhere to its essence, hesitated to do away with.

In the absence of communion records and other evidence of membership, we have to rely on the entries in the church register for a clue to the membership of Zion Church in those years. There are several indications that the average member was young, recently immigrated, with almost no family ties. While Pastor Scheib baptized 120 children from 1835 until 1840 (when the conservative members left), between 1841 and 1848 there were seventy-eight baptisms, and from 1849 until 1855 only *eight* children were baptized into Zion Church. The comparative youthfulness of the membership in the forties and fifties of the last century becomes evident from the records of burials: from 1835 to 1840, 85 burials; 1841 to 1848, 34 burials; 1849 to 1855 only 2 burials.

Marriages as recorded by Pastor Scheib in the church register also show a great decline. From 1835-1840 the Pastor married ninety-five couples; from 1841 until 1849, thirty couples.

With so little pastoral work at hand it is not at all surprising that the Rev. Scheib turned his energies to a field of endeavor which was ever dear to him: the education of the youth.

In the preceding chapter we have read what Zion school looked like when Pastor Scheib came to Baltimore. He found, to use his own words, "seventeen miserable little worms, male and female, all in a second-story classroom, having beaten into them the catechism, with some reading, or memorized passages (!), some writing and a bit of arithmetic. On the first floor dwelt the sexton of the church, who was also the official grave digger, burying his corpses as a sideline; on the second floor the schoolmaster held forth, burying the spirits and souls of his little charges as a main line."

One year afterwards, Pastor Scheib transformed what had been a parochial school into a regular primary and secondary school. His plan for reorganization of the institution was readily approved by the Church Council. The new school was set apart from Zion Church. Religious instruction was only extracurricular. Furthermore, Scheib insisted on the use of both English and German in the school, an innovation which met with much criticism, as from the earliest days on, all classes at Zion School had been held exclusively in German. A school-directorium was set up, composed of members of the vestry and other parishioners. On November 1, 1836, the new school opened its gates for the first time. Seventy-one students were enrolled in the first courses.

Soon the number of Anglo-American, Catholic, and Jewish children, together with the children of Protestant German families who were not members of Zion Church, exceeded by far the number of Zion's own boys and girls enrolled in the school. There was only one distinction between members' children and others—members paid a smaller tuition fee. The faculty at first consisted of two good teachers and the pastor himself. As the old school building was too small to accommodate the increasing number of pupils, the church edifice was made available for the classes.

Pastor Scheib brought an entirely new philosophy of education to this school. First of all, he gave the teachers and the parents of the pupils an opportunity to participate in the various affairs of the school. On January 3, 1839, his newly created parent-teacher association (almost certainly the first one of its kind in the United States) met to discuss the future of the school. He set forth his pedagogical principles in a bi-weekly paper, the *Allgemeine Deutsche Schulzeitung,* published in Baltimore in 1839-40.

When the second year began, the total enrollment stood at 94. The final examinations and commencement exercises were conducted in a solemn form each year, and consisted of demonstrations by the pupils, musical programs, and the award of honors. In 1838, a third teacher was secured and the building enlarged. In 1839, a fire destroyed the school building completely. A large new school was built, with bright, well-ventilated classrooms.

Although Scheib's School was absolutely independent and self-supporting except for the ground and the old building, which were furnished by Zion Church, the congregation took much interest and pride in the school. In 1850, the members of the church donated $8,000 to the institution. The enrollment was constantly swelling. In 1853, there were 315 pupils; in 1861, 418 boys and girls were students of the various classes, ranging from kindergarten to the upper grades. The Civil War did not affect the activities of the school, and at the close of hostilities the maximum enrollment was attained—802.

The period from the end of the war until the opening of public English-German schools in the seventies brought Scheib's unique school to its high point of growth. Twenty classrooms, a faculty of sixteen carefully selected teachers, a library and study rooms served the needs of its many pupils from all over the city. The essence of this successful institution of learning, however, was Pastor Scheib's own pedagogical genius. His philosophy of education was far advanced over most of the contemporary concepts of teaching. The first paragraph of the constitution of Zion School concisely expressed his views:

"The intent of the institution is rational education, or the natural development of the faculties lying within the child in order to lay the foundation for personal, social, and general welfare. The essence of this educational method is based upon the following principles:

a. It observes the development of the human being and proceeds in accordance with nature by inciting and exercising in ascending order the powers which slumber within the child.

b. It considers the child as an organic being which develops through external stimuli according to innate laws of nature.

c. Since the human being received no faculty in vain, this method strives for the cultivation of all talents in naturally ascending steps.

d. Since all knowledge originates with experience, this method employs visual aids. It is a demonstrative method.

e. Since the essence of the human being lies in the desire for the realization of the true, the good, and the beautiful, this method is ethical, or moral and religious in character.

f. As man must attain good qualities through his own efforts this method awakens in every regard the independent action of the student."

Proceeding along these lines, the school was eminently successful. Most of the subjects offered by present-day high schools were taught, in a lively manner which aroused the interest of the students. Thousands of Baltimoreans went through Scheib's School, and the influence of Scheib's approach has been evident in their acting and thinking. Many men and women who later achieved prominence in the life of the city and the state were once students at "the school way down on Gay Street."

The school declined in numbers when the English-German public schools were started in Baltimore, and the latter, keenly sensible of the rivalry, ever increased in efficiency. The free tuition of the public schools attracted a large part of the former patronage of Zion School, and finally in 1895, but not until after a long struggle, Scheib's School, because of large annual deficits, was forced to close its doors.

The first ten years at Zion were infinitely hard and trying for Henry Scheib. Only his tremendous energy and his profound faith in what he professed to be the truth enabled him to bear the tribulations of those years. His natural kindness forbade him to be bitter, and yet, amidst vile attacks from many sides, even the best of men would occasionally have rebuked his assailants with fervor.

The most deplorable attacks launched against Zion Church were the attempts to expropriate the congregation. *The Lutheran Observer* in Baltimore published an article in which reference was made to the deed of Zion Church. It spoke of the "desirable property" which should no longer belong to the congregation of Zion, as their pastor had broken with the Lutheran faith. It has been customary with Lutheran churches in this country to give financial assistance to members who form a new congregation, especially if these members originally contributed to the erection of the mother church. If the formation of a new congregation takes place under friendly auspices, such settlement is easy. Members had broken away from Zion repeatedly, the largest number during the pastorate of the Rev. Haesbert, who himself left with the dissenters. None of these members received any financial aid from Zion. Most of them had left before Pastor Scheib came. When he assumed his work at Zion the treasury of the church was at a low ebb. The flood and the burning of the school in 1839, the great fire of 1840, put such a heavy burden on the congregation that any financial support of Lutheran churches organized by former members of Zion was impossible, even though there was some willingness to help.

The congregation stood behind its pastor admirably, in fending off those attacks. The growing reputation of Zion School won Pastor Scheib and his flock the respect of a wide segment of the German and also the Anglo-American element in Baltimore. But there was still an atmosphere of suspicion which surrounded Zion Church. Some members never got rid of the suspicion that two fires (in 1839-1840) had been acts of arson by ill-meaning fellow-citizens. Pastor Scheib publicly discouraged such a belief.

Although still young, Henry Scheib felt the brunt of the manifold troubles; his health was impaired. In 1847, he decided to move with his family (in 1839 he had married Lisette D. Eisenbrandt, the oldest daughter of the well-known Baltimore instrument-builder, C. H. Eisenbrandt) to the country not far from the outskirts of the city, where he had acquired some land and a farmhouse. For seven years he lived the life of the farmer, commuting between the country and the city, where he had to go several days of the week to fulfill his duties as a teacher and preacher. In the year 1855, he was compelled to abandon his farm, as his presence was required in the city at all times.

This was the decade when the foreign-born population in many American cities had to run the gantlet of political rowdies who opposed the enjoyment of equal rights by immigrants. Zion, being an exclusively German immigrant church, was naturally in the center of these nativistic attacks. Many a Sunday, ruffians of the Know-Nothing Party disturbed the services. Picnics of the congregation in city parks were branded as "drunkards' meetings" because the participants did not frown upon the consumption of beer on Sunday afternoons. Rowdies, using sling-shots, bowie-knives and revolvers to intimidate the peaceful gatherings, almost invariably appeared on the scene. The Church Council resolved, one Sunday, to make a congregational excursion to a greater distance by railroad, hoping to remain undisturbed by nativist elements. In Magnolia Park on the east side of the Gunpowder River, Pastor Scheib convoked the congregation for an impressive outdoor service. At the meeting place, a police escort had been provided for their protection. Within a short time a large number of Know-Nothings assaulted the gathering. Police officers and the men of Zion congregation engaged in a bloody fight with the ruffians.

The German element in Baltimore determined to counteract the nativistic movement. Pastor Scheib and many Zion members had an active part in arousing the Germans and other foreign-born citizens of Baltimore to form protective guards. The leaders of the German-Americans decided to stage a political demonstration with the purpose of directing the attention of the native Americans to the share the German element had had in the historical development of the United States. Zion Church, being the oldest German institution of the city, was best qualified to demonstrate how a church could preserve its German character and still be an integral part of American life. On the 2nd of September, 1858, a gorgeous procession of all German congregations, societies and military companies of Baltimore marched through the streets of the city to "Rullman's Garden" on Frederick Avenue. Pastor Scheib delivered the major oration at this meeting, pointing out the patriotism and firm attachment of the Baltimore Germans to the

Zion Church and Scheib's School—1880

political institutions of their adopted country. The demonstration was called "The Steuben Festival" in commemoration of the German share in the Revolutionary War.

This imposing gathering had a twofold effect. The Know-Nothing press became more just and mild in speaking of their foreign-born fellow citizens, and Pastor Scheib, who along with other members of Zion Church (Albert Schumacher, a prominent layman of Zion, was the leading spirit behind the demonstration) had taken such a conspicuous part in it, became henceforth one of the unchallenged leaders of the German-Americans in their political, cultural and social life, a position also held by his successors, Pastors Hofmann and Evers. From the isolation of a heretic and discredited congregation, Henry Scheib had led Zion into the foreground of German-American activities in the city.

Scheib's Church was at long last respected. The liberal Germans who settled in Baltimore in great numbers in the early fifties were attracted by the clear and intellectual preaching of the spirit who occupied Zion's pulpit. Pastor Scheib was not a political man. When the Civil War broke out and Maryland was caught between the two warring factions, his sympathies were with the Confederacy, which for him was not the symbol of slavery but the manifestation of an aristocratic, social order in contrast to the rowdyism so often evident on the Northern side. He was liberal enough to rally his congregation, which was largely pro-Union in sentiment, around him, and he guided church and school through the difficult war years without any mentionable loss.

More and more, Zion Church was able to develop peacefully. Occasional attacks from all-too-eager clergymen could be warded off without abandoning the dignity which alone makes controversy and debate on differences of opinion a gain to both parties concerned. There was, however, one group which waged an unrelenting, bitter campaign against Pastor Scheib and his church. The Missouri Synod, a body of Lutherans that held most obstinately to the old dogmatic orthodoxy, untiringly denounced Scheib's preaching and practices throughout the years.

When, in 1879, the Pastoral Conference of Baltimore, Missouri Synod, inquired into Scheib's practice of baptism, it was told curtly, "Please show the authority which gives you the right to demand a confession of faith from me and which permits you to subject me and the Church Council of my congregation to a court of inquisition. Until such proof has been brought in clear and irrefutable manner I have neither the time nor the inclination for another word in a fruitless correspondence." Whereupon the Pastoral Conference of Baltimore in conjunction with the Theological Faculty of St. Louis condemned Scheib and "his crowd" and warned people against Scheib's baptism. The Conference had 500 copies of its vitriolic declaration printed for distribution. In 1881, the Church Council of Zion published a pamphlet, most likely written by Scheib himself, entitled *Zion Church and the Recent Charges of Heresy by the Baltimore Pastoral Conference and the Faculty of St. Louis,* which closed with these words: "We cannot help but express the wish that when the Pastoral Conference and the Faculty publish their next bull against Pastor Scheib and Zion congregation, they have a very large number of copies printed in order that we too may benefit from it without too much trouble. With this request we take leave forever of these two reverend institutions—the Baltimore Pastoral Conference and the Faculty of St. Louis." This pamphlet also contained a forceful and outspoken explanation of the faith as it was being preached and lived at Zion Church.

"My Christianity is the religion of the intellect, of freedom, of love, in contrast to the religion of the letter, of force, of fear; veneration of God in the spirit and in the truth. Love is the yardstick and the condition for forgiveness and guilt. Free, trusting devotion to God, rising from evil to good, which Christ calls love and faith. The two are inseparable. Belief without love, without joyful willingness, is no faith; and love without faith, without trust, is no faith. Jesus Christ showed mankind the way to God, not through the sanctuary of temples, sacrifices and dogmas but through the holiness of the heart and the conscience.

"The completion of the Kingdom of God is the eternal life. The Kingdom of God begins on earth; the earthly life is the preparation for the heavenly life. The development, the enlightenment of those who are inhibited by earthly barriers, the saturation of the thirst for truth, justice and love, the satisfaction of the longing of the heart, the quest of the conscience—is the aim which the better part of man is already here endeavoring to achieve. The faith in an hereafter enlivens and strengthens the willingness to fulfill the duty, the courage to endure the evils of life.

"This concise statement of my religious views can convince any unprejudiced person that my religion is nothing more and nothing less than the Christianity of Christ. If I have been repeatedly attacked, judged and condemned on the part of the church for it, it could neither confuse me nor embitter me. I have never spoken or written a hard word against my assailants. But I could not stop obeying God more than men."

In his autobiography, which was discovered several years after his death, Pastor Henry Scheib gave this definition of his faith. Throughout his pastorate his theological views were in accord with this statement. By these views he shocked many, when he came to Baltimore; and by these same views, he gathered many into his fold. We would become as guilty of self-styled righteousness as his enemies of the Missouri Synod if we attempted to evaluate his theology in the light and retrospect of the present-day position of the Lutheran Church in America. Henry Scheib was a product of the liberal and enlightened ideas of the 19th century, and he was one of the outstanding and most honest representatives of religious thought of his days.

At a time when the church in Europe began to awaken and to receive new thoughts and critical interpretations with an open mind, the Lutheran Church in America took refuge behind an immovable dogmatism, which, along with other factors, accounts for the loss of many Lutheran immigrant families to the church. When Scheib arrived in America he saw himself confronted with an orthodoxy which was already receding in Europe. He had spent years of serious studies to formulate for himself certain basic tenets of truth and faith. If he was pressed to accept premises which were inconsistent with his fundamental beliefs he reacted violently. He relied solely on the powers of his mind and on the examples which natural science offered, to arrive at the truth. Nothing, not even ecclesiastical doctrines, should step into the way of truth.

If he had needed any confirmation of his views about the effects of obstinacy in holding to orthodox dogmas, the merciless attacks of the Missouri clergy against Zion Church would have furnished him sufficient proof. He was appalled at the bitterness with which Christians fought one another in the name of pure doctrine. He was aware that he had taken over a Lutheran pulpit. His attachment to Lutheranism was a sentimental matter. He felt an affinity to Martin Luther, who had revolted against the abuses of the dogmas of his day. And yet Pastor Scheib in his obvious adherence to rationalism could not be counted as a Lutheran, no matter which divergent views of Lutheran theology we might call upon for his justification.

Professor Albert B. Faust, pre-eminent historian of the German-Americans, a member of Zion Church and a pupil of Scheib's School himself, wrote in his work *The German Element in the United States:* "Under the pastorate of the Reverend Heinrich Scheib, the *Zions-Kirche* departed more and more from Lutheran dogmas, following in the path of the liberal doctrines of the great German preacher, Schleiermacher, and coming close to the position of the Unitarian Church in America." Scheib, however, never considered himself a Unitarian. Although he denied the Trinity, and refused to acknowledge any binding creed, he never went so far as to view the Bible merely as literature or as a history book explaining an evolution in the moral generation of man. He took the Bible down from its position of infallibility, but studied it with an ardent desire to recognize the faith and the inspiraton contained in it.

He was by no means alone in his stand. But he was outspoken and too sincere to conceal his views. This attitude was what made his work so fruitful and his words so powerful. His sermons were masterpieces of oratorical art. His congregation financed the printing of many of the *Lehrvorträge,* as he called his sermons, particularly in 1881, when the controversy with the Missouri Synod reached its climax.

In his sermon preached on March 27, 1881, on St. John 18:37, Scheib drew a masterly sketch of every doctrinal dispute and religious war from the early beginnings of the church until his day. With perfect clarity he named and explained all the doctrinal battles of Christendom, in a sermon which took him hardly more than 45 minutes to deliver. After throwing light on the dark and bloody chapters of Christian history, he concluded with this challenge: "Pray if you want to: I thank thee Lord that I am not like other people. Say grace before every meal. Confess your sins on Sunday. But beware that during the week you do not deny the great soul who admonishes us so earnestly: Love your neighbor, judge him not. Praise the Saviour in the company of the chosen, and when you hear his word, cry with Herod, the parasite: This is the voice of a God and not of a man; but be careful not to strike your neighbor in his face with your right or your left hand in your zeal for the Lord, when he does not join you in the Amen. What is truth? Not religion in this form. Religion is more than a rush of words. Religion is life. Examine yourself whether your life is religion."

Pastor Scheib has inspired three generations with his faith. Among the German immigrants who came to Baltimore between 1840 and 1870, there were a large number who did not adhere to the creed of any church for their moral guidance. He gathered them into his fold and prevented them from joining the millions of unchurched and unbelieving men and women in America. To them he appealed, and he drew them to Christ as a moral guide. It is a testimony to his merit that today we still find the names of numerous descendants of those intellectual German immigrants on the roll of Zion Church and of other Lutheran Churches in the country.

The long incumbency of Zion's pulpit by Henry Scheib after 1840 was characterized by the harmony which he preached so consistently. Before his days, Zion had been a congregation of Sunday Christians. By founding the *Liederkranz* he created the first organization connected with the church which accorded members the opportunity to meet outside of the regular services. His *Bildungsverein,* a cultural association, likewise served the purpose of interesting his parishioners in activities centered around Zion Church and School. After the Civil War the membership increased steadily for a decade. At a time when women took very little interest in active church work, the pastor's wife, Mrs. Lisette Scheib, in 1868, founded the *Frauenverein,* which has since become outstanding among the church organizations of Zion and in times of need and of war has extended its benevolent help in a most generous manner.

Due to his theological views, Pastor Scheib remained isolated among his brethren of the cloth. Men of similar persuasion seldom shared the pulpit with him, even for occasional sermons. Seldom during this period and only for brief terms, were assistant pastors working by his side.

The first of these assistants, the Rev. John C. Hoyer, was

engaged by Pastor Scheib with the consent of the Church Council in 1841. He was a young and extremely capable minister, who had severed his synodical connections prior to his coming to Baltimore. He stayed with Zion until October 1844, when he received a call to Richmond to take over the newly founded German Lutheran St. John's Church. St. John's, the only German church in that part of Virginia, was likewise an independent congregation. Pastor Hoyer carried on his work much as Scheib did in Baltimore.

Throughout the year 1869 Zion again had an assistant pastor, the Rev. Dr. Rudorf, a missionary who had come to Baltimore after fourteen years of service in Australia and the Orient. He had been rejected by the Lutheran authorities for his liberalism and found himself in full conformity with Pastor Scheib's views. His sermons were much acclaimed, but the congregation was reluctant to support two ministers. With the help of Scheib, Dr. Rudorf attempted to found both a church and a school in nearby Washington, patterned after the institutions of Zion. After a brief stay in the Capital, however, he found out that the German Lutherans there did not respond to his persuasions, and he left for the Midwest.

The anniversaries of the Zion School and of Pastor Scheib's services to Zion became, for the congregation, the occasion for the expression of its deep gratitude to its spiritual guide. The noble enthusiasm and the inspiration with which his words were endowed stirred the throngs which filled the church. But to the observer of the every-day life of Zion Church in the eighties it became evident that there existed a distressing gap between the festive occasions and the ordinary life.

Soon the entire life of the church was again limited to the service on Sunday morning. The *Bildungsverein* had ceased to exist; the *Liederkranz* developed into a social singing society. In 1888, Mrs. Scheib died, and much of the work which she had shared with her husband went back on his shoulders. The labors necessary to maintaining the outward life of the church and the personal responsibilities involved in guiding the inner life of a Christian family had become so manifold that it required almost more than the energy of a single individual to give every detail due attention. While other churches in the city provided a wide range of social activities for their members, which especially attracted the younger generation, Zion Church did not keep up with modern concepts of church activities.

Pastor Scheib was growing old. Most of the older members stood faithfully in the ranks, but younger people broke away until there was an almost total absence of young men and women on the church roll. Compared with the hundreds who had once pledged their vows and taken first communion at the altar of Zion, the number of actual members was decreasing constantly. Henry Scheib, saddened by the closing of Zion School, opposed any attempt to introduce a Sunday School. Despite the pastor's warnings that a Sunday School would contribute to undermine what he called the "spirit of Zion," Mr. W. Theodore Schultze of the Church Council and the young assistant pastor, Wagner, founded Zion Sunday School on December 2, 1888. Pastor Scheib never was reconciled to this action. His assistant had to leave after only a few months of service. In the fall of 1889 the candidate Julius Hofmann was called from Germany to assist Scheib. He arrived in December of the same year and for seven years labored under great difficulties at the side of the venerable old man, who, at the last, was growing bitter and stern after his many tribulations. Once again the conflict between young and old broke out, tempered only by the respect for the lone giant who had devoted his lifetime to Zion Church.

For decades Pastor Scheib had borne the whole burden on his own shoulders. Among his colleagues of the ministerial profession in Baltimore he was shunned. This loneliness became especially evident when Pastor Scheib had to perform the funeral rites for his own immediate family, his wife and several of his children, who preceded him in death. Now it was hard for him to share his office with a young man whose views differed to some extent from his own.

Upon completion of his 88th year of age, Pastor Scheib resigned, on November 15, 1896, after 61 years in the pulpit of Zion Church. He died on the same date of the following year. "When the news of his death spread through the city, thousands of people were deeply moved. How much had come to a standstill with the death of this man! How many memories were connected with his life. Gratitude and veneration were the sentiment of the large assembly in the church that had come to mourn his death. On the first anniversary of his death, the congregation and a multitude of friends from all over the city assembled once more, this time to dedicate a monument which they had erected on the burial lot of the Scheib family in Lorraine Cemetery. It bears the inscription: "Truth, Justice, and Love." Among the manuscripts which Henry Scheib left behind, this prayer—completed by the octogenarian after being revised several times over a period of fifty years—was found:

"Upon the foundation of unity and of peace
rests the structure of our well-being.
Unity, harmony of our powers is strength;
Harmony of forms is beauty;
Harmony of thinking is truth;
Harmony of conscience and will is virtue;
Harmony of conscience and feeling is love.
And love of God and man is religion.
That, Father, we seek. For that we pray.
Grant it to us thy children."

CHAPTER FOUR

Zion Church in Recent Times
1896-1955

Wɪᴛʜ ᴛʜᴇ ᴅᴇᴀᴛʜ of Pastor Scheib, Zion Church entered upon the long road back into the communion of the entire Lutheran Church. It moved triumphantly ahead, and if in any matter it turned back, it was only to the simplicity of faith and sacredness of purpose which had inspired the founding fathers of 1755. The tempests of the 18th century, which shook Zion and caused the radical changes from the conservatism of Kurtz through the extreme orthodoxy of Haesbert to the rationalism of Scheib, were outlived. But with the death of the man with whose name the church had come to be identified in the outside world, little remained that promised to be the foundation for a new start. The essence of Pastor Scheib's life and work had been a humanistic open-mindedness, an idealistic readiness to serve and live by faith. This attitude enabled the three pastors who have since held the pulpit of Zion Church to close the ring of the historical progression on which the life of every congregation travels around its center, Jesus Christ.

This most recent chapter of Zion's history, which has been witnessed by most of the members who form the congregation in the bi-centennial year, is not the tale of radical changes. It depicts the gradual growth and harmonious development under the leadership of pastors who did not hold the church in their hands alone but made the congregation conscious again of its role in the life of the church. A young pastor ascending the pulpit of his church for the first time may be full of plans for radical changes, but he will soon find himself confronted with the long, venerable tradition of yesteryear. To progress without neglecting a great tradition was the task of those who succeeded Scheib.

Pastor Julius Hofmann clearly saw this challenge before him

when he preached his first sermon to Zion on January 5, 1890. But the realization of most of his plans had to wait. His zeal and eagerness to intensify the congregational life was greatly dampened by the senior pastor, Henry Scheib, until 1896. Thanks only to his self-imposed restraint and his personal respect for his elder colleague, young Hofmann succeeded in preventing a breach, which up to this time had always accompanied the transition from the pastorate of the old minister to the ascension of the pulpit by a young successor. Still, we can appreciate a statement by Pastor Hofmann: "These were the six hard years."

Julius K. Hofmann was born on April 9, 1865, at Friedberg in Hesse. He received his theological training at the University of Giessen. After coming to Baltimore, he enrolled in courses at The Johns Hopkins University. His was a deep and comprehensive education, combining the best elements of German scholarship and American practical knowledge. After he succeeded Pastor Scheib, he returned to Europe to marry Miss Adele Chatin of an old French-Swiss family, a union which was ever a source of inspiration for him throughout his life, broadening his outlook and adding much of the heritage of French culture to his personality.

He drew a keen sketch of Zion Church as it presented itself to him when he began his pastorate: "There was the moment when everything declined. Church and school were affected by this fate: within two decades they had become forms with a shrunken content. The children had no understanding of the value of the liberty through which the parents had been freed. They joined other congregations, where every deserter from Zion was received with great joy as if a heathen had repented his sins. It was the time of the rumor that we believed in nothing."

He was determined to give the empty form a content which would again justify the use of the name "Lutheran" by the congregation. The rationalism of Scheib was not alien to him, but he was well aware that its day had been outlived when he wrote: "The nineteenth century opened with the revival of the Gospel by Schleiermacher. With him both Rationalism and Pietism became antiquated, and wherever they reappear, they are but a residue of a by-gone age.

"In the course of the nineteenth century, through the labors of the historians and the theologians, the interpretation of the Gospel, which was God's gift to Martin Luther, was more deeply understood and more extensively made the criterion of the criticism of the literature and the dogma of the church. The Lutheran Church has gained new insight into the foundations of its belief and has been inspired by new confidence in its mission. At the present, more than ever, the Lutheran Church is able to understand and to appreciate the motives that led to the Reformation and moved the reformers to give us those admirable documents among which the Augsburg Confession stands unexcelled."

Pastor Hofmann also laid down the principles which guided him in tackling the problem of changing the services at Zion, which had been made into "lecture services" of a secular nature by his predecessor: "The service also, both in its order and in its guiding principles, shows the tendency towards a closer conformity with that of the beginning of the sixteenth century. The character of secular amusement has gradually vanished from the sacred Sunday hour, and the discussion of the topics of the day has given place to a sermon, which strives not so much to utter and to explain the doctrines of religion as to give religion itself. Sunday worship thus has been made indispensable to the cultivation of spiritual life, and the church plays an ever-increasing part in the life of its members."

Within one decade, the Rev. Hofmann successfully transformed Zion Church along these lines. With great tact and understanding he prevented the older members from opposing him, and gained the support of the small group of younger people who had stayed with Zion. Soon the number of young members on the roll increased, and those whom he had confirmed seldom broke away. Many an older member who had threatened to leave Zion Church upon the death of Pastor Scheib became reconciled with the young pastor.

The difficulties confronting Zion were not only of a spiritual nature. The question of reorganization had been delayed from year to year. The clearance of the lot on Lexington Street had imposed a heavy debt on the treasury of the church. The original deeds, containing clauses regarding the property of the church which prohibited the sale of ground and allowed its use only for purposes of worship, again presented a problem. A congregational meeting on the question of disposing of property brought no results.

Although the young assistant pastor had the support of John Boring, the president of the Church Council, no action could be taken. All who were concerned with the reorganization faced the difficulties of this transitional period, when the old ideas were still deep-rooted and the new had not yet been sufficiently formed.

With the election of Wilhelm T. Schultze as president of the Church Council, a movement for a new constitution got under way. Both Pastor Hofmann and Mr. Schultze prepared the text of the constitution, which was accepted by the congregation in May 1892. Without any radical changes, for which the time was not yet ripe, it introduced the following new provisions:

For the first time in Zion's history the women of the congregation were allowed to participate in the election of the preacher.

The amount of the regular contributions was left to the discretion of the members, a minimum of five dollars a year enabling them to vote.

The Church Council, which so far had consisted of elders and vestrymen, was reorganized. Only one type of councilman was created. The office of the trustees was abolished and their duties transferred to the Church Council.

The enactment of the new constitution during the lifetime of old Pastor Scheib made it the more valuable an instrument for Pastor Hofmann when he became the sole leader of the church. Also during the decade between 1890 and 1900, the question of the deeds was solved through the untiring efforts of Adolf Simon. The minutes of the Church Council of these years bespeak the labor of this man in disentangling the church's disadvantageous legal position. The president of the Church Council, Wilhelm Schultze, finally succeeded in having the restricting clauses of the original deeds annulled by the Maryland Legislature.

Now Pastor Hofmann could concentrate on the spiritual life of the congregation. Beginning in March 1891, he had edited the *Kirchenblatt,* in which he explained his stand. Ever since, the *Kirchenblatt* (later *Gemeindeblatt,* now *Monatsblatt),* has proved a valuable instrument by means of which the pastor, the Church Council, and the various church organizations have remained in close contact with all the members of the church.

The worship service received the form which still survives today; and, although it deviates considerably from the Lutheran liturgy, it constituted an important step forward when we consider the formless style of Pastor Scheib's "lecture services." Young Hofmann found it difficult in the beginning to convince the congregation that the singing during the service was not aimed at achieving top musical quality, but should be an expression of common praise and prayer. For many decades congregational singing had been neglected altogether. Many of the well-known Protestant hymns were unfamiliar to the congregation.

The old hymn book *Neuestes Gemeinschaftliches Gesangbuch,* printed in New York in 1850, which contained over 650 hymns, many of them antiquated, proved entirely inadequate. In March 1893, Pastor Hofmann began the compilation of a new hymnal. Shortly after the death of Scheib the work was ready to go to the printer. The hymn book committee, under George Bunnecke, John Hinrichs and Robert M. Rother, advised the pastor during the six years' work of preparation, and Zion's own hymnal was introduced on the occasion of the Christmas service in 1899. It was largely based on the *Gesangbuch* for Alsace and Lorraine and contained about 200 hymns. In 1902, a second edition was published, which to the present day has remained in use in the German services.

The *Kirchenmusikverein,* founded by Hofmann in 1894, furthered choral and folk music and helped greatly to embellish special services. It found most of its members among the youth of the congregation. Also in 1894, the *Deutsches Liederbuch* was published by the Sunday School, truly a pioneer work, as the publication of non-religious songbooks was just in its initial stage in this country at that time.

The Sunday School, of which we have spoken in the preceding chapter, widened its influence upon the youth of Zion Church, and now the first adult class was founded. Many families who had left Zion Church or simply lost interest in their membership were approached by the pastor and a group of members in an evangelization program. By 1908, Zion Church had 650 members on its roll, many of them young people who took part in the manifold activities which the renewed congregation provided. With the creation of the *Gemeindeabend,* a monthly fellowship meeting of the families, the pastor successfully countered the tendency of a great number of people to limit their social life to one of the many German societies in the city, instead of participating in church endeavors.

The holidays of the church year were observed by beautiful special services. Communion was no longer offered to the men and women separately, as had been the tradition for so long, but the family now went together to the altar of the Lord. Reformation Day was observed annually. To honor the memory of Pastor Scheib, the annual *Kirchtag* was celebrated on October 18. From 1904 on, outdoor services were held once a year, the well-known Zion *Waldandacht,* an observance which was extremely popular in Germany at that time.

Zion Church Library was founded and developed into a remarkable collection of valuable works on the history of the church, on the German element in the United States, and on German and English literature.

Under Pastor Scheib, Zion Church had been viewed by the other German Protestant Churches of Baltimore with indifference, suspicion, even hostility. A gradual change of the church's position was brought about with much patience and in the spirit of neighborliness. Pastor Hofmann sought the fellowship of his colleagues and soon won their respect. When Zion Church celebrated its 150th anniversary in October 1905, for the first time in several generations the ministers of its sister churches took part in the memorial service.

Amidst this revival of Zion Church, one question became more acute from year to year: most of the families had moved away from the old part of the city into the outlying districts. New churches were founded in those sections, a circumstance which made it tempting for many German families to join them instead of going downtown every Sunday morning for the services at Zion. Time and again the floor was open for debate on the question of whether the church should be located in some other part of the city. Even Pastor Hofmann, for a while, was in favor of choosing a new, permanent location for Zion.

The great fire of February 7, 1904, threatened to spread to the church. The roof of the school house caught fire during the Sunday morning service, and the congregation had to be dismissed. In the evening the roof of the church itself caught fire and burned in two spots, but the precautions which had been taken prevented any considerable damage. The Church of the Messiah on Fayette and Gay Streets was completely destroyed, as were many other edifices in the neighborhood. When the Messiah congregation began to rebuild their church on the same location, Pastor Hofmann wrote in the *Gemeindeblatt* in March 1905: "Not a few of our members are now wavering in their conviction that we should move, since Messiah Church is being rebuilt on the same spot where it was destroyed by the fire of February 1904. Well, but the fact that they are building there does not mean they are not committing a mistake. If they make a mistake it is not necessary for us to make one."

The congregation was divided on the issue. Although many favored the removal of the church into another section, most of them feared that the financial burden would be too great. The sentimental attachment to the venerable old building, whose walls had endured almost a century, also played a role in the discussions. "Then the downtown church is doomed" was a common slogan, and more than once Pastor Hofmann was told: "Just wait, it won't be long and there will be a sign on the door of Zion Church: For Sale." But those who wanted to keep Zion on the old location finally prevailed. Pastor Hofmann himself was won for the idea.

In February 1903, he had submitted suggestions for fundamental changes in the interior of the church, but when the question of a possible removal came up, he withdrew them, hoping for an entirely new building. Five years later his original plans were taken up again and realized within a few months.

The redecoration of the interior was carried out according to the pastor's plans. It is a testimony to his artistic taste and conception. Every section of the walls, every touch of color had its meaning. "It is one of the unforgettable experiences of my life that my congregation feels like me about our church. May I say what I endeavored to create? Without making essential changes I wanted to create a space in which the old simple gaslight and the stoves with their long black pipes would be bearable. Now, they don't hurt any more, they belong there. Secondly, everything should be genuine: no imitations of marble. It is simple, painted wood. The color was demanded by the shade of the wall, which should reflect a friendly quiet light in the morning hours. The iron pillars which bear the *emporen* were covered up, for the naked iron was cold and sober."

Three designs from his own hand were the only decorations: the rose of Christmas as the symbol of joy, vines and ears of grain representing the Last Supper, and olive and oak branches, symbolizing "Evangelic" and "German."

In the center above the altar he placed the man who brought evangelic faith back to men: Martin Luther. The painting of the reformer is a copy of the Luther portrait by Lukas Cranach. It was painted by William C. Rost, a member of Zion Church.

All this work was completed in time for the celebration of the 100th anniversary of the erection of Zion Church. But Pastor Hofmann's plans went further. After it became certain that Zion was to remain in the heart of the city despite all temptation to move the church, he conceived the idea of adding a *Gemeindehaus* (parish house). There was much opposition at first. Most members abhorred the idea of going into debt for something that the church had gone without for such a long time. But through the foresight, zeal and genius of the pastor, even the most critical men and women were finally convinced of the importance of the project.

For Pastor Hofmann, the congregational life apart from the Sunday services was of utmost significance. Many new members, immigrants like all the generations before, needed a focal point for their social and spiritual life. If Zion Church could provide a home for this life, they were won. Their children would be won, too. With a rare vision he recognized the advantages which the location of Zion offered for such an undertaking. City planners were full of schemes to convert the ugly space eastward of the City Hall into a Civic Center. Discussion dragged along for years. All kinds of fantastic plans were designed. Some wanted to pattern the square upon the Place Vendome of Paris; others were for the erection of grandiose monuments. Pastor Julius Hofmann did not wait for the decision of the city planners.

He was often seen pacing back and forth, making sketches, taking notes. After a while he summoned an architect and went to work on the civic center himself. He made a small-scale model of the parish house as he had conceived it. Theodore Pietsch, his architect, presented the estimate: a staggering amount. In 1909 the pastor submitted plans and estimates to the Church Council. After some deliberation, the Council approved the project unanimously, expressing an enthusiasm which reminds us of the men who

JULIUS K. HOFMANN
1889-1928

carried out the building of the church in 1807-08. The Council, however, made one condition: the amount of $25,000 had to be in hand before the construction could be undertaken.

With much ingenuity pastor and congregation went to work. From 1910 until 1912, an annual sale and exhibit was held, designated as *Leipziger Messe,* which turned out to be a popular fair. By 1912, $7,187 had been raised during the three fairs, and the sum augmented by gifts, subscriptions and contributions to $45,551. In the same year the cornerstone of the Parish House of Zion Church was laid. In 1913, it was completed.

Built of red brick in the Hanseatic style, its tower inspired a well-known writer to exclaim: "This is the German cathedral of Baltimore." With its arcades and the low-walled garden at the northeast corner of Holliday and Lexington streets, it was the first part of the beautiful Baltimore Civic Center of today. For Zion, the Parish House has become the tangible evidence of the inherent strength, ambition and right to existence of the Lutheran congregation which located here 200 years ago, along the marshy meadows of Jones' Falls. In the years past, during two World Wars and during peace the *Gemeindehaus* has been a thing of incalculable value to the very life of the church.

Pastor Hofmann sent to Germany for the three-bell chime that hangs in the tower. He commissioned his friend Hans Schuler to carve an eagle for the parish hall entrance: the American eagle with a shield on its heart depicting the German eagle—a symbol of the German immigrant at the heart of America. The pastor himself took a hand in interior decoration and painted the walls of the room designated for the smallest children.

When the Parish House was opened, a mortgage of $35,000 was still to be paid. There was much fear that the load was heavier than the congregation could bear—but on November 9, 1924, the debt was finally paid, and Zion rejoiced with its pastor on that memorable day. But the decade between the opening of the *Gemeindehaus* and the liquidation of the final debt was the most trying period in the history of Zion Church: World War I.

Not since the founding of the First English Lutheran Church in Baltimore by former members of Zion, had the language issue come up—not for almost ninety years. There was no question

The parish house and parsonage built 1912

about the German character of Zion Church. Waves of immigrants from Germany poured into Baltimore. The founding of the German Empire in Europe had increased the racial consciousness of the Germans in America. At the turn of the century there were more than thirty congregations in Baltimore which had Sunday services in German. When the German immigration subsided somewhat during the first decade of this century, many German churches readily introduced English services, which gradually supplanted the German altogether.

German-Americanism, as we call this phenomenon of two generations ago, puzzled many observers. Most of these Germans in Baltimore were law-abiding citizens, and nobody actually questioned their loyalty. At the same time, however, they seemed to take such an alert interest in their old homeland that unknowingly they created the impression of being Germans first and Americans only second.

Zion Church had been German since its inception. Nowhere in Baltimore was an organization to be found where the spirit and the outer life were more genuinely patterned in the Teutonic style than in the old church on City Hall Plaza. Pastor Hofmann's name appeared on the roll of most of the German societies. He was a much-sought-after speaker at rallies of the German-Americans. Members of the church were to be found everywhere in the activities of Baltimore's Germandom. John Tjarks, the prosperous hotel owner and faithful son of Zion, for ten years headed the Independent Citizens' Union, a group of German societies that constituted a potent political power in Baltimore.

When the World War broke out in Europe in August 1914, there was no question where the sympathies of the German-Americans stood. The awareness that the motherland was engaged in a life-or-death struggle at once prompted them to prove by acts of charity their attachment to the Old Country, where fathers and brothers were fighting for the Fatherland. Pastor Julius Hofmann, who was active in the National German-American Alliance, placed the Zion Parish House at the disposal of the German-Austrian Red Cross Aid Society. Prior to 1917, almost a million dollars was collected for German and Austrian war widows and orphans, the congregation of Zion having contributed a considerable share of this amount. In the *Adlersaal* of the Parish House a

German eagle was "nailed," each nail bringing a contribution for the war victims in the Old Country.

These activities were observed by the non-German public with much distaste. Gradually public opinion tended openly toward the Allied cause. The entry of the United States into the war against Germany became more and more probable. The enthusiastic feeling of the German-Americans, who considered themselves the hyphen between Germany and America, "the living demonstration of the fact that a large population may be transplanted from one to another country and may be devoted to the new fatherland for life and death, and yet preserve a reverent love for the old," as Carl Schurz once expressed it, greatly disturbed those who foresaw the war between the two countries.

In the midst of this situation, when the feeling ran high, Pastor Hofmann remained calm and sober. He never wavered in his profound faith in the values of his German heritage and culture, but, untiringly, he reminded his congregation of their oath of allegiance to the new country. In 1916, when he was serving as the Chaplain of the House of Delegates, he introduced English vesper services, which henceforth, for many years, were held regularly in the Parish House. This gesture of preaching in the language of the country attracted many Anglo-American hearers and convinced them that Zion was not a secret bulwark of the Kaiser.

On Good Friday of 1917, when a state of war between the United States and Germany was declared, there was no longer any doubt as to the loyalty of the people of Zion. Again it was the Parish House where hundreds of helping hands assembled—the Patriotic Helpers of Zion Church, and the Liberty Loan Drives, Zion Branch. Despite personal tragedy and torn hearts, surrounded by suspicion and often by hatred, Zion's people fulfilled their duties. For the soldiers who spent days or weeks in Baltimore before being shipped overseas, Zion opened its hospitable doors.

After the end of the war, Charles H. Miegel thus characterized his pastor's attitude during these years of storm and stress: "Pastor Hofmann was a great inspiration during the trying years. No opponent of his, however prejudiced or ignorant, can but admire this —that the man and his congregation performed sternly and loyally their duty as American citizens without prostituting the ideals of their Lutheran Christianity, and without surrendering one iota of

FRITZ OTTO EVERS

1929-1952

Pastor Emeritus since October 1952

that proud inheritance of our Germanic traditions as expressed in language, in literature, in learning, in music, and especially in our religious tenets. It was an heroic achievement, indeed—great because it was accomplished through glorious and mighty effort."

Many sons of Zion were in the Armed Forces. Four of them did not return. A cross of wrought iron, standing between the graves of the old pastors in the church garden, was erected in their memory.

The life of the church went on. The attendance at the services often was small. The stress on the members was too great. Racial hatred did not stop at the doors of the churches and schools. But when the pastor sent out an appeal to all members to return to the church for the Christmas service of 1918, he preached on Christmas Day to a church which could not have been fuller in the easy years before the war. What was most important, the youth remained faithful to Zion.

Expressed in numbers, Zion had lost some of its strength. Spiritually the church emerged stronger from the ordeal. The congregation had grown together in the face of hostility. It had also survived as a German church, soon remaining the only church in Baltimore where German was preached every Sunday. In the *Gemeindeblatt* Pastor Hofmann laid down his attitude toward the language question: "No prejudice, no refusal, and above all no hatred for the English language. Use it for your communication as you use money. The language is the medium to reach people: the more you master, the better it is. Therefore the Hebrew New Testament was lost, but the Greek which appealed to the world was preserved. But as we do not fight the English language we must demand that we be left alone, too. We should try to preserve our German way of looking at things and attempt to improve it by foreign factors. We are and we remain an American church of the German tradition. The German Gospel as interpreted by Martin Luther is and remains ours. We live on the impulses which it conveys."

The first steps forward, when peace was again established, was the building of a new parsonage to conform with the old world style of the Parish House. Immediately after the armistice, Zion Church began to raise funds for the relief of thousands of destitute Germans—strangers as well as friends and relatives. Through the

Lutheran church relief, Zion was drawn closer to the entire church. The Lutheran Inner Mission accepted the hospitality of the congregation and for many years held its annual lenten services in the Parish House, services in which many renowned Lutheran pastors preached.

The founding of the *Church Club* in 1920-21 was another proof of the reviving life in the congregation. Increased attendance, the liquidation of all debts through the willingness to help of all members from the richest to the poorer ones, and manifold activities around the church forged Zion's people together. Amidst all these efforts stood Pastor Hofmann, his hair grey now, but his spirit seemingly unaffected by the trials through which he led his people.

To mention the whole scope of his work in the church, in the city, but also in the state and well beyond its borders, would require more space than this history can devote to him. The generation whom he baptized, confirmed and led on to life is present today in every endeavor of Zion Church. In their faith and in their actions his ministry is still evident. The buildings, the garden, the books, which his great mind devised and placed at the heart of Zion, bespeak the achievements of the man who served Zion for almost forty years. There is hardly one nook or corner at Zion where the touches of his hand cannot be sensed even today.

He continued the proud independence of Zion Church, of the *Freikirche,* but gently led his congregation toward a closer fellowship with the Lutheran Church at large. He banished rationalism from the pulpit and substituted for it an almost romantic, childlike faith which filled the hearts of his people with charity and kindness. When he rose to preach, his figure had something of the stature of the Reformer Martin Luther, whose picture above the altar gave Zion a rare distinction among the Lutheran Churches. Pastor Hofmann's liturgy—his own creation, like so many other things— instilled a longing for the mystery of Christ which remained ever alive among the congregation.

For many new immigrants after the First World War, Zion provided a spiritual home and a harmonious introduction to the new American homeland. *Bund Neuland,* for many young Germans who came to Baltimore, was the first anchor they set in the unknown sea of America.

In spring 1927, the pastor went to Germany to recover from a serious illness. At the University of Giessen, which had conferred upon him the honorary degree of Doctor of Theology, he lectured and was enthusiastically received by the students. After his return from his old homeland he resumed his duties, which had been taken care of by the Candidate of Theology Heinrich Falk during his illness and absence. A few weeks later he collapsed at the altar of the church while instructing his confirmation class. On the next morning, May 19, 1928, he closed his eyes forever.

The congregation buried him under the linden tree amidst the works which he created. His grave is marked by the beautiful and simple monument from the hands of his friend Hans Schuler.

We now enter the most recent period in the history of Zion Church, a period which has been witnessed by most of the present membership. We do not yet have sufficient distance from the events for an evaluation—but the facts alone will attest that the present generation is worthy of those who built and lived, believed and sacrificed to insure the continuous existence and growth of Zion Church.

After a brief interregnum which was filled by Pastor August Bauer of Thuringia, Germany, the congregation called the pastor of Zion Church in Philadelphia, Fritz Otto Evers, to Baltimore. On January 27, 1929, he was installed as the regular pastor of Zion. Born in Berlin on August 25, 1886, he was trained at Kropp Seminary near Schleswig for service with the German Lutheran Church in America. In 1908, he arrived in New York, and was ordained in July of the same year at St. John's Church in Englewood, New Jersey, where he served as pastor until 1912. While in Englewood he married Luise Clara Micho. After two years of service as Director of the Lutheran Emigrants House and as Immigrant Chaplain on Ellis Island, he followed a call to the pastorate of Zion in Philadelphia in November 1914. For fifteen years he led this venerable congregation, which was founded in 1742 by Henry Melchior Muhlenberg.

With the experience of a long pastorate at a church so similar to Zion in Baltimore, Pastor Evers was well equipped to continue the great heritage of Pastor Hofmann. The illness and absence of his great predecessor had left many scars, which had to be healed by untiring efforts. Within a short time the congregation had again reached its old height. Pastor Evers was granted permission to maintain membership in his Synod, and the clause of the constitution which expressly forbade synodal membership to the pastor as well as to the church was amended to that effect. Thus from the outset of his twenty-four-year pastorate, Pastor Evers remained in close contact with his Lutheran brethren in the pulpits of other churches. For Zion this fact proved beneficial and did much to help remove the old prejudice against the "chains of the synod" which dated from the days of Pastor Scheib.

Pastor and Mrs. Evers filled the parsonage with the exemplary life of a German *Pastorenfamilie*. Fifteen years ago when a newspaper correspondent visited Pastor Evers, he drew a sketch of the man whose work has meant so much to Zion: "The pastor is a gentle, kindly man with a sweep of long gray hair that distinguishes him in the midst of any company. Alone in his *Sakristei,* in a velvet housecoat, a long cigar in his fingers, he is definitely a part of Zion Church."

Not only were the institutions which he found when he arrived in Baltimore continued, expanded and enlarged, but he ventured to create anew much that had been lost—and this during a time when many voices predicted the final doom of the German church in America. In 1929 the German Language School opened with a broadened scope, restoring the scholastic tradition of Zion Church, which dates back to the first schoolmaster, Moritz Wörschler. The school met with an unexpectedly large response. In the thirties it reached an enrollment of over 220 pupils. Miss Elsa Conradi, who was the principal of the school for many years, also wrote a delightful textbook, which was introduced in German schools in many countries. Never in the twenty-six years of its existence has the school lacked voluntary teachers; among these was the pastor's wife.

The Julius Hofmann Memorial Foundation, a memorial to his predecessor, was created to further the interest in German instruction in the public schools. Each year the foundation awards books and medals to outstanding students of the German language in Baltimore.

In 1930, Zion celebrated the 175th anniversary of its founding. The church was completely redecorated, without, however, impairing the character which Pastor Hofmann had given it twenty years before. Between the high holidays of the church year and the special festive occasions, Zion's life went on in manifold ways. The outdoor services were repeated every summer. Even a service in Low-German was once held for those who had come from Northern Germany.

A dream long cherished by Zion's people came to be realized in 1934. Through the generosity of Ferdinand Meyer, who left a bequest of $50,000 to his church, it was possible to create an endowment fund to assure the permanency of Zion Church in the future.

The peaceful development of the church was once again interrupted when the Second World War drew near. Again Germany was the enemy, and many younger immigrants had to go through the same hardships and pain which a generation before had had to endure. One hundred and fifteen men and four women of Zion answered the call to the colors. A special committee ministered to these servicemen and women in a spiritual as well as material way throughout their service. Five of the heroes did not return from the battlefield and the seas.

At the home front, the congregation concentrated on the war effort. Unforgotten is the day in May 1942, when Pastor Fritz O. Evers on behalf of Zion Church committed the ambulance "The Pioneer" to the hands of the American Red Cross as "the gift of Zion Church for the work of mercy and in honor of Dr. Charles Frederick Wiesenthal." The gift was accompanied by a considerable check for the purchase of blankets. As during the First World War, the Parish House was again opened to servicemen on furlough, on all weekends, for lodging and a breakfast on Sunday morning. More than 15,000 men were accommodated from 1942 until 1945.

Every Wednesday the "Zion Church Group working for the American Red Cross," composed of many women, met to sew and knit for the soldiers. The regular work of the congregation was not impaired by these additional activities. All these challenges resulted only in a firmer union and closer understanding among the members.

After the end of the war when the boys returned home, there was no respite from these additional tasks. The war had spread poverty and disaster over many regions of Europe; Germany especially was suffering from its aftermath. Zion Church joined without delay in the relief work of Lutheran World Action. Money, food, and clothing were contributed to an extent which excelled any previous effort of its kind.

ZION CHURCH COMMITTEE FOR LUTHERAN WORLD RELIEF

Contributions, June 1946 to December 8, 1954...... $26,148.54

Disbursements to December 8, 1954:

Lutheran World Relief (LWR)......$	7,000.00
Lutheran World Action (LWA)......	2,885.00
"CARE"—249 packages to Europe...	2,490.75
Drugs, medicine, etc................	156.09
Express charges on 235 cartons of food, clothing, to Easton, Pa...........	112.57
Cord, cardboard containers, wrapping paper, etc.	406.44
Dry cleaning, repairs to shoes, etc.....	342.57
Printing, stationery, stamps, etc.......	514.43
Purchases of finished materials........	3,393.61
Purchases of unfinished materials......	1,531.99
Purchases of food..................	2,738.93
Postage on 2188 packages (30,671 pounds) to Europe........	4,072.89
Expenses—"Waldandacht," Sunday, August 7, 1949..........	164.10
Miscellaneous	176.46

Total Disbursements to
December 8, 1954..................$25,985.83 $25,985.83

Balance as of December 8, 1954.................. $ 162.71

CONRAD ZIEGET, JR.
Chairman and Treasurer,
Zion Church Committee for
December 8, 1954   *Lutheran World Relief*

This share in the common effort of all Lutheran Churches in America again strengthened the bonds between Zion and the

Lutheran Church at large. Frequently pastors of other churches came as guest preachers. While thus growing more and more into the fellowship of the whole church, Zion has not neglected its special task, which the founding fathers so clearly defined: to be a German church in America. What little was left of the once abundant cultural life of the German element in Baltimore centered around Zion. Pastor Evers, in spite of a severe illness, made preparations for the Goethe Celebration in 1949. Although this event was postponed until January 1950, Zion was on that date the host to one of the most impressive demonstrations of cultural values which the German nation has contributed to the world.

Quietly, something was happening at Zion which would have caused a storm of protest a few decades ago: English services were introduced at intervals and finally became a regular institution. In these days immigration has practically ceased altogether. The great Atlantic migration is a thing of the past. There will always be some newcomers, but the prophecy of Wiesenthal that "our children, almost entirely, learned and understood the English language quicker and better than our German tongue, and in the case of many there was even reason to fear that the language would be lost entirely and the religion with it" has finally, at least as regards the language, become true for the last German bulwark in Baltimore, Zion Church.

From the beginning of the year 1949 a serious and painful illness had greatly impaired the working capacity of Pastor Evers. Lest the church suffer from his impediment he recommended the calling of a co-pastor. Thereupon in September 1951, the Church Council called the Rev. Leopold W. Bernhard of Brooklyn, N. Y. to Baltimore as co-pastor of Zion Church. On October 21 of the same year, the new co-pastor was installed by the Rev. J. Frank Fife, President of the Maryland Synod.

For one year both pastors shared the work at Zion. On September 21, 1952, Pastor Evers informed the congregation during the Sunday service of his desire to resign:

> "For long golden years I have enjoyed the love and the confidence of my Zion congregation. I was permitted to give to her the mature years of my life. With all my love I have dedicated myself to all her work and service at all times in a joy-

ful spirit. During the most trying days of my life the praying heart of the congregation has upheld me.

"Today I stand at a point where I am filled with serious concern about the future. My physical ability to carry on in full measure the many-sided duties of my office has been greatly diminished. No one knows how true this is in the measure in which I myself know it.

"I wish to leave a congregation as united as Zion under God has stood with me in dark and in bright days through all these years. Peace and unity are the foundation of healthy and God-pleasing congregational life. Now all of us, and to a heightened degree, have only this one task: With utter disregard of all our personal wishes and plans, doubts, concerns and prejudices, everyone in Zion must now do his part in loyalty and with earnestness to preserve unity and peace within our ranks.

"The hour has come for me when with a quiet heart, though with deep regret, I recognize and accept the fact that my retiring from my office at this time is a necessary, and therefore good decision, for the welfare of my beloved Zion Church to which I will remain loyal in all gratitude as long as I live."

On October 19, 1952, the congregation presented him with an honor scroll which expressed some of the gratitude and affection of the people whose spiritual leader he had been for almost twenty-four years which said in part:

"As pastoral shepherd Pastor Evers has planted in the hearts and homes of his people confidence and faith in God. He has rejoiced with those who rejoiced; and he has brought comfort to those who mourned. With the Word of God and with the power of his personality he has given human souls direction and has surrounded them with his friendship and his love.

"Pastor Evers' sermons have lifted up the spirit of his congregation. They remain in their beauty, power and depth an unperishable part of Zion's history.

"As fascinating teacher Pastor Evers has molded the heart and the character of numerous young people and has prepared them for the battle of life.

LEOPOLD WILHELM BERNHARD
1951-1954

"Pastor Evers remains for us a shining unforgettable example.

"In recognition of his working and of his being, Zion Congregation therefore confers upon Pastor Fritz O. Evers the honorary title of Pastor Emeritus."

Of his many contributions, the issues of the *Monatsblatt* and his masterly sketch *Zion in Baltimore* betray, more than a resolution of his congregation could express, the true man, Fritz Otto Evers. Wherever his pastoral work took him, in Englewood and New York, at historic Zion of Philadelphia, as a chaplain to the House of Delegates, as a member of the Board of American Missions of the United Lutheran Church, and among the German-language groups all over the country, he has gained the love and respect of all.

Two years in the history of a congregation which stands at the eve of its bi-centennial celebration are but a very brief span of time. Yet, the time between October 1952, when Pastor Bernhard assumed the sole spiritual leadership of Zion Church and November 1954 when he left has been full of events which can only be understood in the light of history, and without recording them this history would not fully convey the consequential course which the congregation has taken during the two centuries of its existence.

Pastor Leopold Wilhelm Bernhard was born in Berlin, Germany on June 15, 1915. In 1933 he began his theological studies at the University of Berlin, where he was soon associated with the then-forming Confessional Church. Because of difficulties arising from the interference of governmental authorities with the life of the church, he went to Zurich, Switzerland, to complete his education. Upon his return to Germany in 1937, he was advised by the leaders of the Confessional Church to go abroad to serve the Lutheran Church there, instead of making a hopeless attempt to work in Germany. In 1938, young Pastor Bernhard arrived in America. At the Biblical Seminary in New York and the Lutheran Theological Seminary in Philadelphia he did graduate work which familiarized him with American church life.

While at the seminary in Philadelphia he helped to copy and translate the diaries of Muhlenberg. In 1941, he wrote with Kress-man Taylor the account of the situation of the church in Germany,

Until That Day, which was serialized in nation-wide broadcasts. Before coming to Zion in Baltimore he served as the pastor of the following churches: Honterus in Gary, Indiana; Zion in Cohocton, New York; Calvary in Jersey City, New Jersey; and Zion (Erasmus Street) in Brooklyn, New York.

Pastor Bernhard's background in Europe, which was formed by the unfearing, militant *Bekennende Kirche,* those Lutherans who did not bend under the pressure of the State, and his excellent training at American seminaries seemed to qualify him eminently as a successor to the pulpit of Zion, which throughout its 200 years has been occupied by men of extraordinary calibre. When he took over his office he found a congregation willing to follow him. The need for a reorganization was evident everywhere. What was more important, however, Zion Church was ready to return publicly to the confessional premises of the Lutheran Church and, only a logical consequence, ready to join hands with the Lutheran Church at large by renewing its membership in the Synod. For 114 years of its 200 years' history, Zion Church had lived as an independent congregation, although the last decades had brought about a close cooperation with the general church in many respects.

Beginning with the October 1952 issue of the *Monatsblatt,* Pastor Bernhard offered a series of articles on the Faith of the Church, which together with his Sunday sermons prepared the congregation for the important decision. He left no doubt that he would serve Zion only if the church became a member of the Maryland Synod of the United Lutheran Church. In his article "Why Zion Should Join the Synod" in the *Monatsblatt,* which inaugurated the fruitful discussion of the subject among his parishioners, he wrote:

"Before I came to Zion I had been given to understand that the Congregation was ready to affiliate with the general Church; I should not have come otherwise. Today I confess freely that I very much desire to be and to remain the pastor of Zion. But I am a pastor, a servant of the Word of God, and that means, a servant of the living Christ. His Will is the highest authority for me; I dare not be disloyal and disobedient to Him. To me it is compellingly clear that it is our Lord's will that Zion live as a member of His Body, His

Church which spans the world. I cannot doubt that as a minister of His Church I must be part of the work of His Church. If Zion will not allow me to be that, I must go where I can be true to Him."

The constitution of Zion Church, which still contained the long outlived rationalistic principles of Pastor Scheib, also needed a complete revision. The many vague statements regarding the faith of Zion Church, the requirements for membership, and the complete absence of any mention of the vital significance of baptism and confirmation called for an entirely new constitution. Here also the pastor led the way for the discussion:

"We claim to be an Evangelical Lutheran Congregation. But our constitution does not say a word about our faith except that Zion shall promote 'rational piety and true ethics based upon the principles of the Gospel.' This definition of our faith does not express a Lutheran or a Christian conviction.

"As Christians we must confess that Christ is our Lord. This was the confession made by those in the days of the Apostles who wanted to be baptized. They had to say: 'Christ is my Lord.' As Christians we must confess the historic Christian faith, and as Lutherans we must state our acceptance of the historic Lutheran Confessions."

The response in the congregation was overwhelming. The Church Council called a congregational meeting for March 23, 1953 in the *Adlersaal*. The discussion and the voting reflected the solemnity of the occasion. The recommendation of the Church Council was first presented by the Council's President, Carl F. C. Schleunes:

"As one who has lived with our congregation for almost fifty years, of which thirty-two years have been given working in Christian fellowship with many true and fine people of Zion, I have gained the advantage of an overall, observant, panoramic picture of the life and faith of our church. Having experienced this kind of church life . . . makes me humbly and prayerfully grateful for this opportunity which brings me before you tonight as your president both of Church Council and congregation.

"I say this particularly because I now have this glorious opportunity to present the recommendation of our Church Council which was accepted only after hard work and conscientious study and which expresses the deepest conviction of my own heart.

"What do we find in close examination of the complete recommendation? We find a greater fullness—a greater fellowship—a greater acceptance of us by other Lutherans of the entire world. We stand together in prayerful worship—in continuous charity and above all at the table of Communion, where we, together with all others, bring the testimony of our Christian fellowship. The appeal I bring you this night—as we stand at the cross-roads of decision is—let us do it together in faith. We must believe the words of our God as He said, 'Try me now herewith—if I will not open you the windows of Heaven and pour you out a blessing that there shall not be room enough to receive it.' "

Henry L. Wienefeld, past president of the Church Council, speaking in German, gave a most vivid description of the history of Zion in the last sixty years, which he witnessed in person, and expressed his belief that the recommendation of the Church Council was necessary for the future growth of Zion and for the continuing effectiveness of Zion's service to German Lutheran immigrants. He pointed out that a united church was standing today as the chief bulwark of defense against the threatening powers of Communism. In order to be true to her faith and her ideals, Zion should be part of that great force of God in the world.

The presentation of the Church Council was concluded by Robert E. Carter: "Our original deeds for the ground on which Zion stands clearly state that they founded an Evangelical Lutheran Congregation, which shall adhere to the unaltered Augsburg Confession. These confessions clearly stated the doctrine and creeds, which are founded upon the Word of God." Mr. Carter then outlined the basic principles of the proposed constitution and emphasized the necessity of the return of the church into the Synod. "We need the fellowship and banding together of the world church to obey Christ's command. The church is the means, the vehicle, the way to participate in Christ's command to us. The Synod is the local part of the greater United Lutheran Church of America."

The Church Council then unanimously recommended the following proposals to the congregation for approval:

    a) That the amendments to the Charter of Zion Church be adopted and that the new Constitution and By-Laws be accepted;

HANS-LUDWIG WAGNER, TH.D.
1954-

b) That Zion Congregation apply for membership in the Evangelical Lutheran Synod of the State of Maryland of the United Lutheran Church of America and authorize the Church Council to effect such membership with the officers of the Synod.

After the vote was taken the results were announced: 651 votes in favor of the recommendation; eight votes opposing, and 121 not voting and therefore counted as opposing. The recommendation was carried with an 83% majority.

The meeting adjourned to the church to give thanks to God. As the congregation stood singing and praying in the old, reverent, beautiful house of worship, a deep, joyous certainty entered the hearts of all who were present that Zion Church will continue in greater strength and in unbending faithfulness in fellowship with the whole church, to the greater glory of God.

Mightily the hymns rang out into the night: "A Mighty Fortress Is Our God" and "Now Thank We All Our God."

This historic meeting of the congregation brought Zion Church a new and lasting foundation for its continued existence. During the annual convention of the Maryland Synod in the Church of the Abiding Presence in Gettysburg, Pennsylvania, on May 26, 1953, Zion Church was received into the Synod. Numerous members attended the solemn reception, at which Pastor Bernhard and the Commissioner of Zion, Carl F. C. Schleunes, were introduced to the Synod by its president, the Rev. Dr. J. Frank Fife.

On June 7, 1953, the festival of the reception into the Synod was celebrated by a great service in Zion Church, at which the President of the United Lutheran Church in America, Pastor Dr. Franklin Clark Fry, welcomed Zion into the brotherhood of the whole church.

After these festive occasions there developed a period of activity which stands unexcelled in the history of Zion. The congregation had to take up its new authority through the work of several committees appointed by the Church Council and augmented by members of the congregation who were not on the Church Council.

The new constitution bases church membership upon baptism and acceptance of the Lutheran faith as outlined in the constitution. Church members are termed active and have the right to a voice and a vote in the congregational meeting if they attend services reasonably regularly, if they voluntarily contribute a reasonable amount to the work of the church, and if they receive the Lord's Supper at least once a year. These provisions necessitated the setting up of an adequate office and record system.

An evangelization program was carried out with much success. In all the church organizations a new impetus was felt. For the first time Zion Church appointed a full-time parish deaconess, Sister Bertha Stickel. Her presence made possible the introduction of a two-year period for confirmation instruction.

In the very center of the life of the congregation stands the living Word of Christ in the worship services, which have been conducted regularly in both the German and the English languages. Traditionally, Zion Church is the German church in Baltimore. Today, as in the past, it is true that the immigrants from Germany are the chief factor in keeping Zion a German church. But the stream of immigration is small and weak. Zion's youth, the children of the immigrants, speak English. By being a truly bi-lingual church, Zion will be able to answer this challenge: to remain the haven for the German Lutheran immigrant and at the same time to provide a spiritual home for his children and children's children.

In June 1954 Pastor Bernhard informed the Church Council that he wished to resign from his pastorate at Zion to accept a call extended to him by St. Peter's Lutheran Church of Manhattan, New York. A special meeting of the congregation was called on July 6, 1954 at which the congregation, with great reluctance, accepted the pastor's resignation.

The historian is still too close to the brief but eventful pastorate of Pastor Bernhard to evaluate it fully. However, there is little doubt in the minds of the church members that his short term had a great revitalizing effect on Zion Church. His Christ-centered church program of evangelization and stewardship gave a new impetus to the congregation. His articles in the *Monatsblatt* and his evening courses clarified for many the fundamental principles of the Protestant faith. His leadership in the problem of re-integration of Zion Church into the Evangelical Lutheran Synod of the State of Maryland of the United Lutheran Church in America has been pointed out on the preceding pages and will always be remembered by the congregation.

Late in September 1954, the Pulpit Committee reported to the

Church Council that it felt fortunate in being able to report that a successor to Pastor Bernhard had been found. The committee recommended the Reverend Dr. Hans-Ludwig Wagner of Chester, Illinois, as the tenth pastor of Zion Church.

On Sunday, October 17, 1954, Dr. Wagner preached in both services as a candidate for the pastorate of the congregation. Following the German service a special congregational meeting which crowded the *Adlersaal* to capacity was held. Upon invitation of the President of the Church Council, the President of the Maryland Synod, the Reverend Dr. J. Frank Fife, presided over this vitally important meeting which was to vote on the unanimous recommendation of the Church Council to call Dr. Wagner as Zion's next pastor. That the President of Synod was invited to preside over a congregational meeting was a truly significant event. For the first time in more than a century, Zion congregation became conscious of its membership in the Synod and the vital help which the Synod was able to give. The voting resulted in an overwhelming majority for Dr. Wagner, who was declared elected pastor of Zion.

Pastor Hans-Ludwig Wagner brings all the qualifications necessary to fill the pulpit of Zion Church. Born in Hamburg, Germany on February 25, 1913 he received his theological training at the Universities of Hamburg, Marburg and Rostock and at the Theological School of Bielefeld-Bethel. He earned the degree of Doctor of Theology at the University of Rostock. He later resumed his theological studies at Saskatoon Lutheran Seminary and the University of Saskatchewan in Canada. Involved in the resistance of the Protestant Church against the National-Socialist regime he left Germany in the year 1938 and emigrated to Canada. He became assistant professor of Hebrew and the Old Testament at the Saskatoon Seminary and at the same time worked for his degree of Bachelor of Divinity. Before coming to Baltimore he served in four parishes: St. Peter, Big River, Saskatchewan (1939-1943); Trinity, Saskatoon (1944-1946); St. John's, Campbell Hill, Illinois (1946-1950); St. John's, Bremen Township, Illinois (1950-1954). Pastor Wagner assumed his new duties at Zion on December 5, 1954. Under his guidance the church will enter the third century of its history.

The two-hundredth anniversary is no end, but a new beginning.

The year 1955 finds Zion Church firmly established on the foundations upon which the pioneers of 1755 built their church. Much has been tried, much has been weighed by the generations of two centuries and proved too light. Untouched remain the immovable foundations of the church of Jesus Christ. Zion Church has closed the ring of two hundred years of history. A mighty fortress of the Christian faith it will continue to strive for the aims which its first constitution, written by the founding fathers in 1769, put forth in touching simplicity: Union with Christ, general edification and betterment of the Christian congregation.

APPENDICES

APPENDIX A

FIRST CONSTITUTION OF THE CHURCH (1769)

Brief Constitution of the Evangelical-Lutheran Congregation at Baltimore-Town, as it was Deemed Necessary at the Time and was Drawn Up. June 10, 1769.

In the name of the Most Holy Trinity

AMEN!

God's ordinance and the nature of public worship which Christians confess require good laws for the church to govern both teachers and hearers. Whenever these do not exist, the service of God can neither be duly held, nor can it be turned by the hearers to their welfare and their union with Christ. General edification and betterment of the Christian congregation is doubtless the only aim of our service of God, which cannot possibly be reached without Christian order. As all members are obliged to edify their own souls as well as those of the others and to prefer always the welfare of the whole congregation to their own advantage, they must pledge themselves to observe and preserve a godly order and discipline.

In our Evangelical Lutheran church of this town considerable disorder and neglect of the public service has been noticed. It is therefore necessary to remedy and to prevent to some extent this evil and all evils of the future and all threatening abuses. Considering this, the following rules and regulations are prescribed as a short church order, carefully deliberated upon and accepted by the congregation and intended for everlasting observance:

I. As Christian order requires many functions which cannot be demanded of the regular preacher without injury to his office, it is necessary that there should be elected from the members of the congregation three or four men, i.e., as many as shall be deemed necessary and worthy at the time, and who are of good faith and unblemished conversation, to serve as permanent elders, as long as they shall continue of an upright conversation. Their names are to be entered upon the church register. It shall be their duty to strive after an edifying conversation and to attend to the functions entrusted to them with zeal and faithfulness, and to be helpers to the preacher in the wholesome administration of his office.

II. Order requires that every year two deacons and trustees be elected by the congregation. No member has the right to refuse to accept such office— not even the deacons in office, if reelected—except in case of insurmountable obstacles. These shall have supervision over church order and discipline and over the members of the congregation and their conduct. They shall provide carefully the necessaries of life of the preacher and shall see to the preservation of public worship, and be faithful therein.

III. It is proper that the deacons who have well served should be publicly discharged of their office and that those newly elected should be publicly presented to the congregation, and be reminded by the minister of their duties, the faithful and conscientious fulfillment of which they shall promise by answering yea!

IV. Once a year on a fixed day the minister shall call the meeting of the congregation according to the desire of the elders. The congregation is obliged to appear at the place designated for the meeting to examine the accounts of the church.

V. Both deacons shall for the sake of order give account to the elders in presence of the congregation. These accounts shall annually be entered in a book and be read by the preacher in church.

VI. In all cases where there is anything to be brought before the congregation, a motion or a complaint, the congregation shall appear at the time and place which the preacher sets and announces.

VII. All complaints arising in the congregation, either against the preacher or the elders, or the deacons in office, or against a member of the congregation, shall for the sake of order be reported to the elders in love and modesty. These, after consultation and with the consent of the preacher, are entitled and obliged to investigate the same and to settle all discord in kindness.

VIII. All members of the congregation must see to it that peace and harmony shall be carefully preserved. Accordingly, no member shall be allowed to separate from church and congregation without grave responsibility and to sever his connection with it on account of some defect or abuse that may have crept into the church as into any society, or on account of certain deficiencies which one or the other member may show, in order that all disorder and discord be prevented in the congregation.

IX. No member of the church shall be allowed to make new rules of his own accord or to change the old rules or to abrogate them without the knowledge or consent of the congregation.

X. All members of the congregation shall, for the sake of equity, consider themselves obliged to pay quarterly the money subscribed by them as part of the salary of the minister, to avoid causing the minister unnecessary and unjustified work. To that end it shall always be duly announced by one of the deacons on the last Sunday of the quarter after the service, in order that everyone may be able to prepare himself. Every Christian should duly consider the rule observed by St. Paul with the Corinthian congregation, I. Cor. ix: 5-7, and should obey it in order that he may do everything necessary for maintenance of the preacher and the service of the church, not with compulsion, or with avarice and unwillingly, but voluntarily, cheerfully, heartily, and for the sake of God's love, for the Lord loveth a cheerful giver.

XI. It shall be the duty of the deacons to collect the Sunday offering every Sunday and holiday at the morning service. No member shall neglect "to do good and to communicate," considering that every mite will well be repaid.

XII. It has been decided for the benefit of the congregation that each and everyone who wants to be buried in our graveyard and to that end has a grave dug shall pay to either of the two elders for a person of 12 years the amount of 2s. 6d. and above the age of 12 years 3s. 6d. In order that everything be done in good order, a grave shall not be opened until it is announced to the schoolmaster or one of the deacons, that they may know and record the person who shall pay for the grave and show the place where the grave is to be made.

XIII. It is for the sake of order very necessary that all members who intend to take Holy Communion in due time and at the proper place, at least one day before confession shall give their names to the regular preacher; these names should be written down and the persons be reminded of the importance of their intention. Their conduct and Christian character shall be inquired into. Their number shall be announced after the sermon. Those, however, who live in hatred and enmity with others or have anything against their neighbors shall appear one week before, in order that the parties may be reconciled either by themselves or in the presence of the preacher or, where it is necessary, also in the presence of the two deacons, in proper time and in Christian spirit.

XIV. Those who through gross and shameful sins give offence to the Christian congregation shall be excluded from Holy Supper until they publicly do penance and promise to make peace with the congregation, in order that all scandal be removed and the other members may learn to fear such sins and to guard themselves against them.

XV. The minister in office shall enter in the church record the time, the year, and the day of those born, baptized, and buried, and shall announce the number of them on New Year's day.

Now, all those that do not agree with these articles, and separate from public worship and from the congregation shall not be considered as members of the congregation, and shall be deprived of all rights and privileges of our church, and of all use of the Holy Sacraments, nor, to their disgrace, shall burial in our church-yard be accorded to them.

All members of the congregation have herewith pledged themselves to the faithful keeping and to lasting observance of these articles, and have subscribed to the same with their own hands.

June 10th, 1769, Baltimore Town.

Carl Wiesenthal	Johannes Schrand	Nicolaus Heimer
Georg E. Lindenberger	Wilhelm Rauch	Mathäs Brechtle
Christian Diel	Peter Strinbock	Joh. Georg Herrmann
Wilhelm Hackel	Friedrich Kirst	Wilhelm Schwarz
Wilh. Löble	Jacob Brown	Johannes Hermann
Johannes Schrimm	Sam. M. Dent	Feydel Rock
Philipp Littig	Tobias Renner	Ludwig Werdenberger
Andreas Rothaug	Joseph Miller	Moritz Wörschler
Heinrich Blechroth	Johannes Breitenbach	Samuel Messer Smith
Johannes Hahn	Engelhardt Jaiser	Johannes Fürst
Friedrich Kohl	Peter Trombohr	Jörg Löble
Mich. Eltrerbach	Jörg Fass	

(On pages 69-73 of the old record book entitled Kirchen-Archiv, *Pastor Kirchner wrote down this constitution in 1769).*

APPENDIX B

ZION CONSTITUTION OF 1773

Articles for the government of the Evangelical Lutheran Congregation in Baltimore Town in Maryland, unanimously agreed upon for the present time until in the future a more detailed constitution shall be adopted.

1. Whereas Christian order in all congregations requires many a function which the regular teachers and preachers cannot fulfill without disadvantage to and interference with their office, it is necessary that in addition to the five elders already in office three other efficient men of good faith and good conduct should be elected by the majority vote of the members in good standing of our Evangelical High German congregation of this town. They should be presented and sworn in publicly and their names entered into the church records. These elders shall consider it their duty both to be of a commendable conduct themselves and to administer the duties incumbent upon them zealously and faithfully. They should be willing helpers for the regular pastor and the teacher, helping them in the salutary ministration of their offices for the congregation.

Out of these eight men also, a treasurer, i. e. a collector and bookkeeper of the revenues of the congregation, shall be selected. He shall give to the others the required bond and shall never keep over 10 or 15 pounds in hand.

2. From now on every year several new deacons shall be elected in place of those retiring after two years' service, and in case one should refuse to accept voluntarily this burdensome office, he should compensate the congregation by a considerable fine. The treasurer and 4 deacons annually, at a certain time, shall give account of their books to the trustees and elders as deputies of the congregation. The state of these books shall be publicly announced to the congregation, and thus suspicion and calumny will be avoided everywhere. Furthermore, these present rules shall be read to the congregation once a year and new members shall subscribe to the same.

3. In all cases where an important matter is to be decided upon, and for which the presence of the whole congregation is deemed necessary, the latter, when summoned by the regular teacher, shall make its appearance duly and willingly.

4. All important and lawful complaints arising in the congregation, either against the preacher, an elder, a trustee and deacon, or against any member, must not be dragged about in the town or in the country, nor indeed be spread out among strangers, but for the sake of order the elders should be notified in charity and modesty. These, together with the regular teacher, are entitled and obliged to investigate the matter and to adjust the difficulties with kindness and in peace, in order to preserve the best peace and welfare of the congregation.

5. All members must see to it that peace and concord, so necessary to the church, are carefully preserved. Accordingly, no one without grave responsibility on his part should withdraw from it on account of some shortcomings or

abuses that creep into the church as into all societies, nor on account of certain faults or deficiencies of one or the other member; in order that all disorder and disruption be avoided and remedied.

6. Neither a single member nor several members are allowed to make changes of their own accord, or to suspend the old rules. All laws of the church and all rules are made with the assent of the regular teacher by two-thirds of the elders, trustees, and deacons, carefully and conscientiously, being attorneys of the congregation.

7. All members of the congregation who, in accordance with the terms of the deed, want to have rights in the church and its property, the church-yard, and other privileges, must voluntarily pay proportional dues towards the maintenance and support of the church, rightly and honestly.

8. At all public services the ordinary offering—as it is customary with all our evangelical congregations in North America—shall be collected by the elders during the singing of the hymn after the sermon, and be counted afterwards, and the amount entered in a special book and handed over to the treasurer.

9. For the burial of strangers in our church-yard not less than 30 shill. specie shall be paid. In case of poor co-religionists a reduction may be granted.

10. Each member shall in due time advise the pastor concerning the baptism of children, burial of the dead, and participation in the Holy Communion, in order that the Teacher may be enabled fully to perform his duties and in order to settle all quarrels peacefully and in time.

11. All gross sinners who by public shame and vices would give offense shall be dealt with in mercy and earnestness according to the teachings of Christ (Matth. V and VI). The same shall, for the time being, be excluded by the pastor from Holy Communion and sponsorship until they show repentance, betterment, and reconciliation with the congregation.

12. These short rules and regulations for the church may in the future, of course, be changed, improved, and augmented according to new conditions, conscientiously and prudently, as divine grace and providence will show and teach us.

We have pledged ourselves to this discipline and to the following articles, of our own accord, with our hand and signature in Christian good faith, viz.:

Carl Fr. Wiesenthal	Jörg Löble	Joh. Friedrich Kies
Wilhelm Löble	Georg Gärtner	Adam Rohrbach
Moritz Wörschler	Joh. Leonhardt Jacobi	Michel Hättinger
Georg Lindenberger	Christian Frölich	Joh. Christoph Grundig
Johannes Schrimm	Johannes Delcher	Johannes Machenheimer
Jacob Braun	Philipp Grace	Peter Machenheimer
Jacob Eichelberger	Carl August Kirst	Christoph Wunder
Lorens Steller	Carl Gottlob Schwartz	Johannes Paul
Vitus Hartweg	Hans Georg Dietman	Philipp Bernhard
Carl Gertz	Heinrich Augustin	Mich. Elterbach
Joseph Miller	Valdin Schneider	Daniel Barniz
John Thile	Jacob Schneider	Georg Thoel
Gabriel Liwyn	Joh. Wilhelm Rauch	Michel Schreyack

Johannes Schronck
Johannes Küffer
John J. Myer
Heinrich Sinmund
Engelhard Yaiser
Johannes Leypold
Franz Friedrich Betz
Erasmus Uhler
John Tinges
Christoph Raborg
Daniel Bender
Adam Gantz
Leonhard Karg
Peter Frick
Philipp Wohner
Friedrich Wille
Andreas Hertzog
Johannes Bock
Adam Kremmer
Johannes Beitenbach
Michael Krosh
Adam Bross
Michel Hättinger
Gottfried Kohl
Nicholas Haller
G. Th. Walckersdörfer
Friedrich Alter
Christian Pauly
Wilhelm Clauer
Heinrich Ziegler
Peter Schmidt
Mathias Rauch
Jacob Mayer
Georg Frank
Georg Reinicker
Peter Littig

Johannes Haan
Matthäus Müller
Michael Krebs
Christi Bachmann
Georg Reisinger
Henry Doyel
Adam Clackner
Philipp Doyel
Andreas Eckel
Jacob Neumann
Georg Leitner
Theobald Klein
Ludwig Stotz
Jerg Reichli
Jeremias Ehne
William Rehberg
Thomas Tool
Johannes Schwinsiger
Johannes Lauer
Bory Jentz
Johann Reiff
Jacob Dieter
Jacob Nusser
Martin Bandel
Dewalt Kremer
Georg Dowig
Martin Sommer
Heinrich Schultze
Martin Breitenbach
George Cole
Heinrich Tuchhardt
Andreas Erppolt
John Cole
Abram Franck
Andreas Schättli
Michael Schorr

Conrad Bauer
Adam Breitemäler
Johann Alter
Johann Rock
Joh. Görg Eberhard
Joh. Georg Nieppert
Leonhard Tassler
Andreas Knauer
Johannes Beck
Philipp Harman
Wilhelm Bauer
Heinrich Zimmerman
Michael Nüchterlein
Martin Bauer
Jacob Grünwald
Friedrich Höflich
Friedrich Klein
Johannes Staub
Solomon Heims
Jacob Block
Christian Meyers
William Choplow
Henry Wineman
George Levely
Samuel Mayer
Henry Harshman
Henry Gantz
Michael Ernst
Andrew Block
R. Dunn
Andreas Hoffman
Friedrich Shaffer
Joh. Martin Bandell
James Davidson
Charles Snyder

(The Constitution of 1773 was entered on pages 36-42 in the manuscript record Kirchen-Archiv).

APPENDIX C

SOME NOTES OF HISTORIC INTEREST

PASTOR BAGER: The oldest chronicle of Zion Church, *Kirchen-Archiv,* states on page ten that Pastor Bager was "high in years" when he left Baltimore. This is evidently an error. In 1763 Pastor Bager was thirty-eight years old. He served afterwards for many years in New York and Pennsylvania and died sixty-six years old on June 9, 1791.

PASTOR KIRCHNER: There has long been confusion about Pastor Kirchner's activities after he left Baltimore in 1762. The Church Records at Friedensaal (Schuster's) Church in York County, Pennsylvania, were kept by Kirchner from January 23, 1763, until December 6, 1767. From his will (Will of John Caspar Kirchner, Office of the Register of Wills, Baltimore County, Maryland, Book 3, Folio 162) it is evident that he had settled in Maryland again by 1768.

PASTOR GEROCK: The tombstone on Pastor Gerock's grave in the church yard gives the date of his death as October 25, 1788. From all sources available it must be concluded that this date is not correct. Gerock died one year earlier on October 25, 1787.

LEWIS BUICHLE: Between the years 1798 and 1802 a silversmith by the name of Lewis Buichle was a member of Zion Church. He was probably born in Germany. It is not known when he came to Baltimore. For a while he had a shop at 4 Baltimore Street. The two flagons in the beautiful Communion service of Zion Church bear one of his marks (LB in Roman letters in a rectangle). The chalices, patens and ciborium, while not marked, were probably also made by him. In 1802 Buichle left for Europe. Other silversmiths among the early congregation were Wilhelm Hackel and Philip Benjamin Sadtler.

PASTOR HAESBERT: Johann Peter Haesbert was born in Cleveland, Ohio, in 1807. In 1845 he became pastor of the Evangelical Church in Hamburgerberg, Rio Grande do Sul, Brazil, where he died in 1890. Cf. *Hundert Jahre Deutschtum in Rio Grande do Sul, 1824-1924* (Porto Alegre, 1924), 471.

APPENDIX D

CONTRIBUTORS TO THE BUILDING FUND OF 1806

Baltimore, Sept. 15th, 1806

To the Members of the Lutheran Congregation.

For a long time it has been the desire of the vestry to build a new church as the present one does not offer sufficient space. As every member of this congregation will easily realize the necessity of a new church edifice, the vestry herewith again appeals to the liberality of the members who have proved their willingness to help on previous occasions.

Donations 'from other friends of the church will be accepted with thanks and with the prayer that God may bless them abundantly in return. Subscriptions may be paid in instalments as soon as the building should be begun.

The names of the subscribers:

Peter Frick
Erasmus Uhler
Georg Dowig
Heinrich Schröder
Repold und Waesche
Friedrich Hammer
Friedrich König
Karl Bohn
Albert Seekamp
Conrad Steinecker
Christian Capito
Johann Ries
Peter Sauerwein
Philipp Horn
James Zwisler
Philipp Itzge
Georg Steinecker
Heinrich Keerl
Johann Leypold
Pet. Arn. Karthaus
Conr. Schultz
Joh. Hauptmann
Andr. Koch
Johann Conrad
Joh. Machenheimer
Joh. Ad. Knott
Nick. Hoffmann
Pet. Bensen
Ludw. Lambert
Joh. Heyl
Jak. Hoffmann
Christian Stever
Joh. Fischbach
H. A. Wilms
Jak. Galleg
Wendel Michael
Friedr. Kummer
Eva Robison

Karl Diehl
Phil. German, jun.
Peter Maurer
Antonius Grovermann
G. Warner
Johann Allbright
Maria Allbright
Wilh. Krebs
Mich. Warner
Friedr. Eiselen
Ignat. Stever
Heinr. Nagel
Jak. Glaser
Martin Bauer
Andr. Block
G. Cole
Joh. Than
Andr. Westrom
Daniel Rieber
Jak. Möllinger
Heinr. Ziegler
Joh. Ziegler
Augustin Schutt
Heinr. Bauer
Dan. Pauly
Heinr. Willey
Maria Willey
Friedr. Mann
Wilhelmine Griepenkerl
Sophia Hoburg
Dan. Dieffendörfer
Josua Howard
Johann Rusk
Joach. Rusk
Joh. Keller
Jak. Schimmik
Mich. Hättinger
Schultze, Consul

Justus Hoppe
Wilh. Räborg
Salomon Heims
Conrad Eiselin
Ludwig Brantz
David Bixler
Joh. Ilgenfitz
Aug. Tegtmeyer
Joh. Heinr. Ewaldt
Carsten Neuhaus
August Schwatka
Jak. Geissendörfer
Ernst Fanth
Heinrich Winter
Joh. Stierly
Georg A. Baursachs
Brinsinger
Heinrich Altvater
Wilh. Schartel
Joh. Steinbeck
Johann Schönberger
Joh. Friedr. Gebhardt
Heinr. Hauptmann
Christian Rindt
Heinr. Rindt
Chr. Heinr. Augustinus
G. Rohrbach
Peter Wigant
Conr. Schrot
Nicol. Emich
G. Capito
Cath. Hoss
Ludwig Michael
G. Kaylor
Joh. Friedr. Bensemann
Sam. Ford
F. Wisotzky
Matth. Hufnagel

Joh. Christ. Kaminsky
Friedr. Haubert
Jak. Schott
Mathias Hermann
Daniel Wagener
Phil. Schwarzauer
Carl Schröter
Karl Morneweck
Friedr. Leypold
Joh. Schrun
Bernhard Struthoff
David Friedrich
Sabina Graff
Dorothea Bayley
M. Elgert
Joh. Peters Witwe
Karl Formann
Georg Daft
Witwe Phil. Schmith
Ehrenfried Nokler
Dominik Frank
Joh. Supper
Ludw. Kandelhardt
Cath. Armstrong
Müller
Mrs. Bandel
Johann P. Strobel
Joh. Schneider
Wilh. Eschberger
C. Diederich Klocke
Adam Boss
Joh. Friedr. Nix
G. Bandel
Philipp Allbright
C. Machenheimer
Christine Delscher
Mich. Kipplinger
G. Pauly
Elis. Schneider
Cath. Claridge
Bernh. Weber
Abraham Knüpp
Ludwig Reppert
Friedrich Brauer
Georg Reppert
Jakob Reppert
Michael Schorr
Joh. L. Alhausen
Wilh. Just. Alhausen
Joh. Merfeld
Jak. Lubstine

Joh. Mich. Dosch
Christoph Müller
Georg Schnauber
Kath. Felly
J. H. Säumenig
Theobald Fauss
Hermann Niemeyer
Friedr. Crafft
Heinrich Schaumberg
Joh. Theod. Kall
Joh. Hanauer
Diedrich Wolf
Wilhelm Keilholtz
J. C. Rau
Joh. Mattais
Joseph Schmid
Heinr. Fouse
Dorothea Forleng
Joh. Keller
Salomon Aulberts
Cath. Milteberger
Joh. Knodt
Cath. Pechin
Aug. Zeumer
Karl F. Meyer
Heinr. Dukehart
Joh. Howser
Caspar Fahs
Pet. Strulbuck
Valentin Drawbach
Georg Benner
Phil. Jatler
Martin Sommer
Heinr. Scheithauer
Zachar. Tensfeld
Caspar Schmid
Joh. Steinforth
Joh. Everson
Dan. Wallander
Joh. M. Rudenstem
Wilh. Warner
Elis. Barney
Joh. Breitenbach
Christian Meyers
D. Gisler
Jak. Eberhardt
Joh. Fischbach
Christian Horn
Jak. Bayfeld
Phil. Myers
Joh. Fusselbach

Jak. Horn
Joh. Lightner
Mich. Lightner
Elis. Brown
Caspar Weber
Friedr. C. Graf
Christian Mayer
Simon Becker
Friedr. Prill
Jak. Miller
Martin Kräber
Friedr. Brendel
Heinr. Böckle
Labes & Co.
Friedr. Brock
H. H. Häckemann
C. F. Kalkmann
H. Heidelbach
G. C. Müller
F. W. Brune
Andr. Glock
Jak. Diel
Thom. Henning
Benj. Henning
Herm. Fricke
Karl G. Börstler
Ludw. Tegtmeyer
Phil. Ackermann
Valentin Waggener
Nikol. Link
G. Lightner
Jakob Seitz
G. Neippert
G. Ackermann
Jakob Mödinger
Valentin Delscher
Conrad Reili
Joh. Dobler
Conr. Grafe
Dietrich Herold
Christian Kaufmann
Christ. Weisshampel
Joh. Wiggard
Cath. Hildebrand
Friedr. Grebe
David Horn
Jakob Small
Wright & Price
Jakob Amigh

(This list, compiled by Pastor J. Daniel Kurtz and written on pages 52-61 in the manuscript record book of Zion Church, is preserved in the Church Archives.)

APPENDIX E

CONSTITUTION AND BY-LAWS OF 1953

PREAMBLE

In the name of the Father, and of the Son, and of the Holy Ghost. Amen.

We, members of the body of Christ, desiring to manifest the inner unity which we have with one another in the common confession, maintenance and defense of our faith in Jesus Christ as God and Saviour, and in joint efforts for the extension of His Kingdom, unite in the adoption of this constitution.

ARTICLE I
Title and Incorporation

The name and title of this congregation shall be "The Zion Church of the City of Baltimore."

This congregation shall be incorporated.

The Services shall be conducted in the German and in the English languages according to the tradition inherited from our forefathers.

ARTICLE II
Doctrinal Basis

Section 1. This congregation receives and holds the canonical Scriptures of the Old and New Testaments as the inspired Word of God and as the only infallible rule and standard of faith and practice, according to which all doctrines and teachers are to be judged.

Section 2. This congregation accepts the three ecumenical creeds: namely, the Apostles', the Nicene, and the Athanasian, as important testimonies drawn from the Holy Scriptures, and rejects all errors which they condemn.

Section 3. This congregation receives and holds the Unaltered Augsburg Confession as a correct exhibition of the faith and doctrine of the Evangelical Lutheran Church, founded upon the Word of God; and acknowledges all churches that sincerely hold and faithfully confess the doctrines of the Unaltered Augsburg Confession to be entitled to the name of Evangelical Lutheran.

Section 4. This congregation recognizes the Apology of the Augsburg Confession, the Smalkald Articles, the Large and Small Catechisms of Luther, and the Formula of Concord, as in the harmony of one and the same pure scriptural faith.

To this Doctrinal Basis all instruction in the Church, the religious school(s) and the families shall be conformed.

ARTICLE III
Of the Synodical Relation

Section 1. This congregation shall be a member of the Evangelical Lutheran Synod of the State of Maryland, a constituent synod of The United Lutheran Church in America, or its successors.

Section 2. This congregation shall consider it its duty to support the

Evangelical Lutheran Synod of the State of Maryland to the best of its ability in the upbuilding of the Kingdom of God.

Section 3. In order to protect the trust placed in the congregation to advance Christ's Kingdom, the congregation, if ever compelled to surrender its charter, designates as heir to its assets, the Evangelical Lutheran Synod of the State of Maryland.

Article IV
Of the Membership

Section 1. Constituents: This congregation shall consist of the Pastor or Pastors and other baptized persons who have been admitted into its fellowship. This Constitution recognizes two classes of members. Child Members and Adult ("Confirmed") Members.

a) Child Members are those who have been baptized and are a part of the family of this congregation, but who have not yet been admitted by the Rite of Confirmation to the Sacrament of the Lord's Supper.

b) Adult ("Confirmed") Members are those who have been duly received into full membership of this congregation by Adult Baptism*, Confirmation, Certificate of Transfer, Renewal of Faith, or Restoration.

Section 2. Duties of Members.

The members of this congregation shall honor God, and seek his gifts of grace by regular attendance upon divine services and by partaking of the Lord's Supper as provided for by the congregation; shall read and seek to understand the Word of God and devout literature in accordance with the Scriptures; shall adorn their faith with a godly life; shall bring their children in early infancy to holy baptism; and shall send them to the Bible schools of the congregation and subsequently to catechetical instruction. In case of illness they shall inform the pastor of the same. They shall live peaceably with one another. They shall greet opportunities of growth in the cause of Christian Stewardship by contributing toward the financial support of the congregation according to their means, and in general seek as much as in them lies to further the life and growth of the congregation, and through the congregation contribute to the general work of missions, mercy, and education as carried on by the United Lutheran Church in America.

Section 3. Classification of Members.

(a) *Active* Members are those who have received the Sacrament of the Lord's Supper at least once within the year, and in the judgment of the Pastor and the Council have reasonably fulfilled the duties defined in Article IV, Section 2, unless hindered by sickness or other circumstances beyond their control.

(b) *Inactive* Members are those who have not fulfilled the requirements for *Active* membership unless hindered by circumstances beyond their control.

Section 4. A *Communing* Member shall be defined as a member ("active" or "inactive") who has received the Sacrament of the Lord's Supper at least once within the year.

---

*A Baptism shall be considered an Adult Baptism, admitting the person so baptized to adult membership in the Church with all the privileges and obligations thereof, when such person at Baptism shall be adjudged by the Pastor and Council as possessing the spiritual and mental faculties necessary to accept personally the privileges and obligations involved in full communing membership.

Section 5. At regular or special congregation meetings all *Active* Members, 21 years of age and over, shall be eligible to vote.

Section 6. Should a member make request for dismissal to a congregation not of the Lutheran faith, the Council may grant such statement of standing as, in its judgment, is just and proper.

ARTICLE V
Of the Pastor

Section 1. The Pastor shall be a minister of the Evangelical Lutheran Church. He shall be a member of the Evangelical Lutheran Synod of the State of Maryland of The United Lutheran Church in America, or shall promptly become a member of the Synod upon his acceptance of the Call by this congregation. Should the Synod refuse to receive him, or should he be deposed from the office of the ministry or otherwise excluded from the membership of the Synod, he shall automatically cease to be the Pastor of this congregation.

Section 2. The election or the acceptance of the resignation of a Pastor shall be by written ballot at a properly called congregational meeting. In these matters, the Council and congregation shall proceed in conference and cooperation with the synodical authorities. The meeting of the congregation for the election of a Pastor should be presided over or attended by the President of the Synod or his representative. At the election of a Pastor, the Council shall nominate only one person at one time and the vote shall be on his election. Two-thirds of the votes cast shall be necessary to an election. When the congregation shall have duly elected a Pastor, the official "Pastor's Call Blank," issued by The United Lutheran Church in America or by the Synod shall be used to extend the Call of the congregation to the Pastor-elect.

Section 3. Should the congregation desire to exercise its right of terminating the contractual relationship between it and the Pastor, this right shall be exercised only after consultation with the President of the Synod, and after the same prayerful consideration has been used that was invoked at the issuance of the original Call, and it shall become effective by a two-thirds majority of all the votes cast by written ballot at a duly called congregational meeting. The meeting of the congregation for the termination of the contractual relationship between the Pastor and the congregation, shall be presided over by the President of Synod or a clerical representative appointed by him for that purpose.

Section 4. The Pastor shall conduct the public worship and occasional services of the congregation according to the principles and usages of the Evangelical Lutheran Church, preach the Gospel, as confessed by that Church, administer the Sacraments, catechize, comfort, admonish the members publicly and privately, and develop in them the sense of the priesthood of all believers.

Section 5. In order that the Pastor may devote himself fully to the duties of his office, he shall receive an adequate salary, paid in regular installments. The amount of his salary and the times of payments shall be specified in the

Call. His expenses incident to attending conventions of the Conference and of the Synod and other general official meetings shall be paid by the congregation.

Section 6. The Pastor shall keep accurate records of all his ministerial acts in the "Parish Register" provided by the congregation for that purpose, which records shall be and remain the property of the congregation. He shall also be the custodian of the official seal.

Section 7. The Pastor or Pastors shall have complete command of the German and of the English languages.

Section 8. The privileges and responsibilities of an associate or an assistant Pastor shall be specified in his Call, which should be prepared in consultation with the synodical authorities.

ARTICLE VI
Of the Council

Section 1. The Council shall consist of the Pastor or Pastors and the deacons.

Section 2. There shall be 15 deacons, *Active* Members of the congregation for at least one year before election, elected by the congregation at its annual meeting for a term of three years. The term of one-third of the deacons shall expire annually. Should a deacon cease to be an *Active* Member of this congregation, or should he without excuse fail to attend three successive, regular meetings of the Council, his office shall at once become vacant.

Section 3. The deacons shall cooperate with their fellow-members and with the Pastor in planning for and promoting the welfare of the congregation. While they shall attend specially to the business and property interests of the congregation, they shall not be unmindful of the spiritual duties set forth by the Church in the office for their installation.

Section 4. The Council shall be the board of trustees of the congregation. It shall see that the provisions of the Constitution and By-laws are obeyed and that the resolutions of the congregation are carried out. It shall arrange and carry out plans for the welfare of the congregation and for its work through the Church at large. It shall guard the order of the services and the purity of teaching both in the pulpit and in the religious school(s) of the congregation. The Council shall be responsible for the employment and supervision of the salaried lay workers of the congregation.

Section 5. The Council shall annually list all Adult ("Confirmed") Members of the congregation as *Active* or *Inactive* Members on the basis of the requirements set forth in Article IV, Section 3, with a view to determining which are in good standing and assisting the *Inactive* Members to improved standing.

Section 6. The Council shall elect from either its own number or the other Active Members delegates to the conventions of the Conference and of the Synod, whose expenses shall be paid by the congregation.

Section 7. The Council shall not buy, sell or encumber real estate unless authority is given at a congregational meeting.

Section 8. The Council shall fill all ad interim vacancies in its lay membership until the next annual meeting of the congregation at which time a successor shall be elected for the unexpired term.

Article VII
Of the Officers

Section 1. At its first meeting in each congregational year, the Council shall elect for a term of one year a president, vice-president, secretary, and treasurer(s). A financial secretary may be elected for a like term. The president and vice-president shall be members of the Council. The secretary and the treasurer(s), if not members of the Council, shall be accorded the privilege of voice without vote in the meetings of the Council.

Section 2. The president shall be chairman of the Council and of the congregation. In the event of the president's inability to perform his duties the vice-president shall serve in his stead.

Section 3. The secretary shall keep accurate minutes of all meetings of the congregation and Council in a volume provided by the congregation, which shall be preserved permanently in the Archives of the congregation. He shall keep all records of the congregation except those provided for in Article V, Section 6, and Article VII, Section 4.

Section 4. The treasurer(s) shall keep all accounts of the congregation. They shall receive the funds of the congregation and disburse them on proper orders, making monthly remittance of all benevolence funds to the proper synodical authorities. They shall make such reports as the By-laws required. They shall furnish bond as required by the Council, at the expense of the congregation.

Section 5. These officers shall be *Active* Members of the congregation. Should they cease to be such, their offices at once become vacant. Such vacancy for causes established shall be officially declared by vote of the Council, and shall be filled by the Council for the remaining unexpired term.

Section 6. Vouchers and checks, after they have been approved by the Council, shall be signed by the president or vice president together with the secretary and treasurer.

Article VIII
Of Discipline of Members

Section 1. (a) If a confirmed member lives in open sin or habitually neglects the means of grace or persistently disregards his Christian duties or repudiates the Christian faith, or engages in persistent trouble-making, especially in the affairs of the congregation, it shall be the duty of the Church Council to exercise church discipline in his case. To this end the Church Council shall have power to cite any member of the congregation to answer charges brought or to give testimony as the case may require.

(b) Discipline shall in all cases be administered after the pattern of Matthew 18: 15-17. The various grades in church discipline shall be private admonition, admonition in the presence of two or three witnesses, citation before the Church Council, suspension or excommunication. The suspension or excommunication of a member shall deprive him of all rights and privileges, except that of attending public worship. Excommunicated or suspended members may have their privileges restored by action of the Church Council, upon the removal of the cause of discipline.

(c) All charges against any member of the congregation must be made in writing and signed by the complainant or complainants. It shall be the duty of the Church Council to investigate and decide such charges. A copy of such charges must be submitted to the accused at least twenty days before the investigation, at which he has been summoned to appear, and at which time he shall be entitled to speak and to produce testimony in his own defense. Appeals from the decision of the Council may be made to the congregation and to the Synod in accordance with the constitution of the synod with which this congregation is connected.

(d) Should differences or contentions arise in the congregation either between the pastor and people, or among the members themselves, and should all efforts to effect a peaceable settlement fail, the matter shall be brought to the attention of the Synod.

Article IX
Of Meetings

Section 1. An annual meeting of the congregation shall be held in the month of January.

Section 2. Special meetings of the congregation for the transaction of proper business may be called by the Pastor or the president of the Council when deemed necessary and shall be called, if requested by the Council or in writing by 50 Active members. In the call for special meetings, the purpose of the meeting shall be specified and at the meeting no other business shall be transacted.

Section 3. Notice of all congregational meetings shall be given by announcement at the worship services on two consecutive Sundays and by mail to all voting members at least ten days prior to meetings.

Section 4. The Council shall hold regular meetings as stated in the By-laws.

Section 5. Fifty (50) Active members at any properly called congregational meeting shall constitute a quorum.

Article X
Of Societies

Section 1. Special interest groups, other than the official auxiliaries of the Church, may be organized only after authorization for such organization has been given to their sponsors by the Council.

Section 2. All organizations within the congregation exist to serve the congregation in its local and world-wide ministry, and as such are subject to the will of the congregation as expressed by the Council or congregational meeting. They shall make annual reports concerning their membership, finances and work as specified by the Council.

Section 3. In case of the disbanding of a society the remaining property of the same shall be surrendered to the Church Council which shall then determine in which manner it shall be preserved or applied.

Article XI
Of By-laws
By-laws may be adopted which are not in conflict with this Constitution.
Article XII
Of Amendments
Section 1. Amendments to this Constitution may be made at any annual congregational meeting by a two-thirds vote of the *Active* Members present, provided that they have been proposed in writing by at least five *Active* Members at the preceding annual meeting, or that they shall have been approved by the Council, and by it submitted to the *Active* Members of the congregation by mail, at least thirty days before the annual congregational meeting.

Section 2. No amendments, however, may be considered which would alter Article II or Article III or Section 2 of Article XII of this Constitution.

BY-LAWS
Section 1—Congregational Meetings
Item 1. The annual congregational meeting shall be held at a time and place to be determined by the Council.

Item 2. At the annual meeting, the Pastor(s), the secretary, and the treasurer(s) of the congregation shall each submit a written report. Each organization and school within the congregation shall also submit a written report.

Section 2—The Council
Item 1. All lay members of the Council properly elected or re-elected shall be installed by the Pastor at the next public service following their election or as soon thereafter as possible.

Item 2. All elections of lay members of the Council shall be by secret written ballot and the result recorded in full by the secretary.

Item 3. Nominations for Council membership shall be made at the annual meeting by the Council. One nominee shall be presented for each vacancy to be filled. Additional nominations may be made from the floor. A majority of the votes cast shall be necessary to election.

Item 4. The Council shall hold regular monthly meetings. Special meetings may be called by the Pastor or the president of the Council on his own initiative. Special meetings shall be called if requested in writing by three members of the Council.

Item 5. The following shall constitute the Order of Business at regular meetings:

a) Devotions
b) A period for the study of the life and work of the Church
c) Roll call and action on excuses for absence
d) Reading of minutes
e) Reception of petitions and communications
f) Report of the Pastor(s)
g) Report of the treasurer(s)
h) Reports of standing committees
i) Reports of special committees
j) Other reports
k) Unfinished business
l) New business
m) Adjournment

Section 3—Standing Committees

Item 1. At the first meeting of the Council in each congregational year the president, after consultation with the Council, shall appoint from its own or from the *Active* membership of the congregation, as many standing committees as the local and general interests of the congregation may require. Members of standing committees shall serve for one year. The Pastor shall have a voice and vote in all standing and special committees of the congregation.

Item 2. The duties of all standing committees not otherwise defined shall be fixed by the Council, from which they shall receive needed instructions. The acts of all committees shall be subject to review by the Council.

Item 3. There shall be a Committee on Church Property. This committee shall provide for the proper maintenance and protection of all property of the congregation and shall see that the same is kept in good repair and adequately insured.

Item 4. There shall be a Finance Committee. If the treasurer(s) is not a member of the Finance Committee he shall have the right to a seat and voice in its sessions. Its duty shall be to prepare the annual budget of the congregation for the succeeding year and to provide ways and means for the gathering of the needed funds in a scriptural and systematic way. The full benevolence budget apportioned by the Synod shall be included in the annual budget. The Committee shall see that the financial affairs of the congregation are conducted efficiently, giving special attention to the prompt payment of bills and to the regular forwarding of benevolence monies to the synodical treasurer. The Committee shall, subject to the approval of the Council, be responsible for the congregation's investments, and shall also provide for the annual auditing of the accounts of the treasurer(s) of the congregation and of its financial secretary, if there be one, as well as the accounts of the treasurers of the organizations and school(s) of the congregation.

Item 5. There shall be a Committee on Worship and Music. It shall be the duty of this committee to assist the Council in seeing that the services of God's house are conducted properly and in accordance with the liturgy of the Church, that competent ushers are provided and that hymnbooks and other devotional helps are provided and properly cared for. It shall supervise the organization and promotion of choirs, be responsible for the care of musical instruments and choir vestments and, in consultation with the Pastor and choirmaster, provide music proper for the services of worship.

Item 6. There shall be a Committee on Christian Education and Literature. This committee, in consultation with the Pastor, shall have responsibility for the organization, promotion and supervision of the religious school(s) and the auxiliaries of the congregation. It shall encourage the use of approved Lutheran literature throughout the congregation, and seek to introduce the Church's periodicals and books of family devotion into the homes of the congregation. The Sunday School Superintendent shall have voice and vote in this committee.

Item 7. There shall be a Committee on Stewardship, of which the benevolence

« 134 »

treasurer, if there be one, shall be a member with voice and vote, and which may include an appointee from each adult and youth organization and the religious school(s) of the congregation. The duties of this committee shall be to promote the expression of the Christian faith in the daily life of the members; to inform them about the congregation's local, national and international ministries; to teach them the Christian use of money; and to lead them to higher levels of proportionate giving for the Lord's work. The committee shall also be responsible for the annual Every Member Visit and other congregational projects which promote informed and grateful giving. *Item 8.* There shall be a Committee on Christian Service having responsibility in the following areas:

a) *Membership and Evangelism:*—revitalizing the indifferent; stimulating and directing the congregation in a continuing program of personal evangelism.

b) *Social Welfare:*—providing a Christian ministry through hospitals, child-care agencies, institutional chaplaincies, services to older people; using and aiding in both church and private welfare agencies.

c) *Social Action:*—studying social conditions, local and national; helping individuals to bring the healing power of Christian truth to bear upon critical problems through discussion of facts and issues.

d) *Emergency Aid:*—bringing relief to members of the congregation and community in times of special need.

SECTION 4—

All meetings shall be conducted according to Robert's Rules of Order—Revised.

SECTION 5—AMENDMENTS

No alterations or amendments to these By-laws shall be made unless they are presented, in writing, to the Council and read at a public service prior to the meeting of the congregation at which they are to be considered. A two-thirds vote of the members present and voting at a meeting of the congregation shall be necessary for the adoption of amendments to these By-laws.

APPENDIX F

ZION CHURCH ENDOWMENT FUND
(As of Summer 1954)

*George L. Wagner	$ 1,000.00
*Dr. Marie Thalwitzer	500.00
Ferdinand Meyer	39,600.00
Henry G. Hilken	1,000.00
Katherine M. Hinternesch	925.00
Johanna Gieseler	1,000.00
William H. Paul	3,622.74
Anna C. Uhrig	2,000.00
In memory of John Uhrig, her father	5,000.00
John G. Maier	5,000.00
William H. Weyforth	500.00
Charles Plitt	203.69
Sarah Bauernschmidt	1,000.00
William Depkin	462.50
Julius C. Brandt, Sr.	250.00
Gustav John	3,150.00
In memory of two members	100.00
Johannes K. A. Tunnecke	100.00
In memory of the parents, Heinrich and Ernestine Leonhardt, Schopfheim, Baden	100.00
Mrs. Louise Scharr	1,000.00
Miss Marie Bernauer	400.00
Carl W. Prior	100.00
Miss Wilhelmina E. Oelsner	200.00
John George Ebelke	1,000.00
†Mrs. Eugenie Schloendorn	500.00
In memory of their parents, Alexander H. and Marie Schulz by the Misses Emma & Alice E. Schulz	1,000.00
‡In memory of their sister, Sophie Schulz by the Misses Emma W. & Alice E. Schulz	500.00
August F. Gieseke	300.00
Emil R. Kreiling	200.00
Bernard Schiphorst	1,000.00
Unnamed Friend	500.00
Mrs. Marie Schneidereith	200.00
†Miss Elsa Conradi	2,883.15
Mrs. Maria Kirchmayer	600.00
†Mrs. Maria Kirchmayer	200.00
1952: Albert L. Heil	500.00
Helen Groneberg	500.00
1953: Margaret Mooyer	3,500.00
In memory of their father, Richard C. Sandlass by Henry L. Sandlass and Mrs. Gertrude Lubke	425.00

*the proceeds are for Memorial Membership.

†the proceeds to benefit the German Language School.

‡the proceeds to decorate Altar on 2nd Advent Sunday.

Acknowledgments and Bibliography

The research for this history of Zion Church was begun in December 1952 and concluded in February 1955. It was undertaken upon the request of the Church Council acting on the recommendation of Dr. Dieter Cunz of the University of Maryland. During the twenty-six months of research and preparations, the assistance of numerous individuals was sought and cheerfully given.

The Rev. Leopold W. Bernhard was untiringly concerned with the project during its every phase. His desire to help and facilitate the research and his warm, personal friendship accompanied the work from the initial stage to the final touches to the manuscript. My friend, Dr. Dieter Cunz, author of many writings on the German element in Maryland and the best authority in the field, accorded much valuable counsel beyond his official capacity as the "Advisor on the Bicentennial History of Zion Church" appointed by the Church Council.

The former president of the Church Council, Mr. Carl F. C. Schleunes, and the Pastor Emeritus, the Rev. Fritz O. Evers, provided helpful suggestions. During the research at the Gettysburg Theological Seminary, Pastor Dr. Abdel Ross Wentz, the historian of the Maryland Synod, gave much of his time and knowledge. Dr. Charles Glatfelder, Professor at Gettysburg College, furnished hitherto unknown information on the early pastors of Zion Church. Mr. David L. Scheidt, at the time a student at the Gettysburg Seminary, assisted in the locating of documents. Mr. Bruno Stein, Editor of the *Baltimore Correspondent,* extended his hospitality and assistance during the weeks of initial research in Baltimore.

Mr. Fred Shelley, Librarian of the Maryland Historical Society, Miss Margaret J. Hort, Librarian of the Krauth Memorial Library, Lutheran Theological Seminary at Philadelphia, and Mr. Paul Swigart of the Library of Congress gave generously of their time in conference and correspondence. Special thanks are due to Mrs. Henry I. Tusing of New Market, Virginia, who made available her large collection of letters written by Lutheran clergymen from 1785-1835. Pastor Edward F. Engelbert of the Martini Lutheran Church, Missouri Synod in Baltimore, contributed material on the Haesbert congregation. Dr. F. Prüser of the *Staatsarchiv* in Bremen, Germany conducted a special investigation to locate records on Pastor Uhlhorn which were of great importance for the respective chapter of this history.

Grateful acknowledgment for extra time and efficient help cheerfully given throughout the months is due to Miss Elfriede Metzler, secretary of Zion Church office. This list of persons who assisted at one time or another in the preparation of this history would be incomplete without mentioning the late Pastor Julius Hofmann, who did more than any other man of Zion Church to preserve and augment the historical records of the church and whose extensive library facilitated the research at every phase.

1) Primary Sources

The records of Zion Church have been the chief source of information for this history. It is gratifying to report that only a few of the records of the church have been lost in the course of time. A systematic search brought to light many documents which were believed to be no longer extant.

The most important record pertaining to the early development of the congregation from 1755 to 1790, with occasional entries covering events up to the year 1830, is the manuscript volume entitled *Kirchen-Archiv, Oder umständliche Beschreibung und Benachrichtigung, des Anfangs der teutschen Lutherischen Gemeinde in Baltimore Town, in Baltimore County in Maryland, und dessen Fortgang*. This manuscript record, which is believed to have been begun by Dr. Charles F. Wiesenthal and subsequently augmented by entries of the Pastors Kirchner, Gerock and Kurtz, was partly published in the original German in: Henry Scheib's "The Zion Church of the City of Baltimore," *SHGM*, ii, 59-72. A complete English translation by Dr. William Kurrelmeyer was published in: Julius Hofmann, *A History of Zion Church of the City of Baltimore 1755-1897* (Baltimore, 1905). All quotations from the *Kirchen-Archiv* follow largely Dr. Kurrelmeyer's translation unless a discrepancy between the original and the translation required a revision.

Zion Church archives yielded a number of other documents pertaining to the early period, such as two ledgers covering the years 1769-1796, bills for organs, building material, and other services, original deeds, notes and letters of the pastors, and subscription lists. For the period covering the last one hundred years, the minutes of the Church Council meetings, and more recently, the complete files of *Gemeindeblatt der Zions-Kirche* and *Monatsblatt der Zionsgemeinde* (1892-1954), pamphlets and programs of services were used.

The minutes of the *Pennsylvania Ministerium* and the *Maryland Synod* up to the year 1835 furnished valuable data on Zion Church and its position with the Lutheran Synods. Other materials were secured by examining page by page numerous volumes of the *Lutheran Observer,* the *Evangelisches Magazin,* the *Lutheran Quarterly,* the *Evangelical Review, Baltimore Correspondent, Maryland Gazette, Baltimore Sun, Maryland History Notes* and other periodicals and newspapers.

Information on the early pastors of Zion Church was gathered from the *Hallesche Nachrichten* (American reprint, Allentown, Pa., 1886), and the *Journals of Henry Melchior Muhlenberg* (Philadelphia, 1945), translated by Tappert, Doberstein, Bernhard, et. alia. A letter by Pastor John Gerock to his son written in 1778 is in the *Maryland Archives,* xlvii, 415 ff.

The Hall of Records in Annapolis, Md., yielded information on Pastor Kirchner *(Register of Wills, Baltimore County,* Book 3, Folio 162), and on the original deed *(Land Records, Baltimore County,* Book A.L.6, Folio 722-726). About the relations of the Lutherans to the Established Church the manuscript *Historical Sketches of St. Paul's Parish* (written in 1855 by Ethan Allen) was consulted in the library of the Maryland Historical Society. Likewise, *Acts of the General Assembly, November Session 1811,* Chapter 134 which contains the act concerning the sale of property by Zion Church.

There was practically no material on the events preceding Pastor Scheib's coming to Zion, in the church archives. The State Archives of Bremen, Germany, and the Zivilstands-Amt of Bremen furnished hitherto unknown facts on the life of Pastor Uhlhorn. Letters concerning Pastors Uhlhorn, Domeier, and Haesbert and the issues of *Der Bürgerfreund* from August 12 to September 16, 1835, in the Krauth Memorial Library of the Lutheran Theological Seminary at Philadelphia made it possible for the first time to describe and evaluate the events at Zion Church between 1830 and 1835.

A complete file of Scheib's *Allgemeine Deutsche Schulzeitung,* his autobiography (Baltimore, 1907), his catechism for Zion Church, sermons, annual reports of Zion School, and the pamphlet *Die Zions-Gemeinde von Baltimore und ihre jüngsten Verketzerer, die "Baltimore Pastoralkonferenz" und die St. Louiser Fakultät* (Baltimore, 1881) were available in the archives and the library of Zion Church.

Printed or manuscript copies of all Constitutions from 1769 until 1953 are preserved in the Zion archives. Programs of the dedication services of 1808 and 1840 are also extant. Numerous devotional and hymn books used by the congregation were consulted, particularly the *Gemeinschaftliches Gesangbuch* (Baltimore, 1817), partly compiled by Pastor Kurtz, *Gesangbuch der Zionsgemeinde* (Baltimore, 1899), compiled by Pastor Hofmann, and *Hausbuch der Zionsgemeinde* (Baltimore, 1905).

2) Published Histories of Zion Church

The following books, pamphlets, and articles on the history of Zion Church are given in chronological order according to their publication:

Kurtz, J. Daniel, "Historische Erzählung von der Entstehung und dem Wachsthum der Lutherischen Gemeinde in Baltimore," *Evangelisches Magazin,* iii (Philadelphia, 1813), 18-21.

Scheib, Henry, *Zur Erinnerung an die Feier des 50. Jubiläums der Zions-Schule, 1886.* (Baltimore, 1885).

Scheib, "The Zion Church of the City of Baltimore", *SHGM,* ii (Baltimore, 1888), 57-73.

Hofmann, Julius, *A History of Zion Church of the City of Baltimore 1755-1897,* (Baltimore, 1905).

Hofmann, *Die Zionskirche, 1808-1908,* (Baltimore, 1908).

Hofmann, *Festschrift Der Zionsgemeinde zum 150. Jubiläum,* Baltimore, 1905).

Miegel, Charles, "The Passing of Scheib's School", *The Sunday Sun* (Baltimore), July 10, 1932.

Evers, Fritz O., *Zion in Baltimore* (Baltimore, 1930).

Evers, *Zion Church, 1755-1945* (Baltimore, 1945).

Snyder, William T., *Baltimore and Zion Church in 1808,* (Baltimore, 1948).

3) SECONDARY SOURCES

Books

ANON., *Baltimore, Seine Vergangenheit und Gegenwart* (Baltimore, 1887).

ANON., *Documentary History of the Evangelical Lutheran Ministerium of Pennsylvania and Adjacent States, 1748 to 1821* (Philadelphia, 1898).

ANON., *Festschrift zur 50-Jährigen Jubel-Feier des Baltimorer Liederkranzes* (Baltimore, 1886).

ANON., *Grundverfassung der Evangelisch-Lutherischen General-Synode* (Baltimore, 1820).

ANON., *Kirchen-Agende der Evangelisch-Lutherischen Gemeinen in Nord-America* (Philadelphia, 1786; Baltimore, 1818).

ANON., *Memorial Volume of the Semi-Centennial Anniversary of Hartwick Seminary* (Albany, N. Y., 1867).

ANON., *Nachrichten von den Vereinigten Deutschen Evangelisch-Lutherischen Gemeinen in Nord Amerika* (Halle, 1787; Allentown, Pa., 1886).

ANON., *Verrichtungen der Evang.-Luth. Synode von Maryland* (Baltimore, 1820).

BEIRNE, FRANCIS F., *The Amiable Baltimoreans* (New York, 1951).

CUNZ, DIETER, *The Maryland Germans* (Princeton, 1948).

EISENBERG, WILLIAM E., *This Heritage* (Winchester, Va., 1954).

FAUST, ALBERT B., *The German Element in the United States* (New York, 1927).

FELLERER, KARL G., *Das Deutsche Kirchenlied im Ausland* (Münster, 1935).

GEROCK, KARL, *Jugenderinnerungen* (Philadelphia, 1890).

GRIFFITH, THOMAS W., *Annals of Baltimore* (Baltimore, 1824).

GUTHE, OSCAR, *History of St. John's Evangelical-Lutheran Church of Richmond* (Richmond, Va., 1933).

HENNINGHAUSEN, LOUIS P., *History of the German Society of Maryland* (Baltimore, 1909).

HOFMANN, JULIUS, *Gedenkblatt gewidmet dem Andenken von Pastor Heinrich Scheib* (Baltimore, 1896).

HOFMANN, *The Germans of Maryland, 1812-1914* (Baltimore, 1914).

JACOBS, H. E., *American Church History—The Lutherans* (New York, 1894).

JACOBS and J. A. HAAS, *The Lutheran Cyclopedia* (New York, 1899).

MANN, W. J., *Lutheranism in America* (Philadelphia, 1857).

MORRIS, JOHN G., *Fifty Years in the Lutheran Ministry* (Baltimore 1878).

MORRIS, *Life Reminiscences of an Old Lutheran Minister* (Philadelphia, 1896).

NICUM, J., *Geschichte des evangelisch-lutherischen Ministeriums vom Staate New York* (New York, 1888).

PLEASANTS, J. HALL and HOWARD SILL, *Maryland Silversmiths 1715-1830* (Baltimore, 1830).

RABB, ADAM G., *Biographical Cyclopedia of Representative Men of Maryland and the District of Columbia* (Baltimore 1879).

ROTERMUND, HEINRICH W., *Lexikon aller Gelehrten, die seit der Reformation in Bremen gelebt haben* (Bremen, 1818).

SCHARF, J. THOMAS, *Chronicles of Baltimore* (Baltimore, 1874).

SCHMAUK, THEODORE E., *A History of the Lutheran Church in Pennsylvania, 1638-1820* (Philadelphia, 1903).

SPRAGUE, WILLIAM B., *Annals of the American Pulpit* (New York, 1869).

TAPPERT, THEODORE G., *The Prospects of the Lutheran Church in America* (Philadelphia, 1945).

TAPPERT and J. DOBERSTEIN, *The Journals of Henry Melchior Muhlenberg* (Philadelphia, 1942).

WARING, LUTHER H., *History of the Evangelical Lutheran Church of Georgetown* (Washington, 1909).

WENTZ, ABDEL R., *History of the Evangelical Lutheran Synod of Maryland* (Harrisburg, Pa., 1920).

WENTZ, *The Lutheran Church of Frederick, Maryland, 1738-1938* (Harrisburg, 1938).

WOLFE, E. J., *The Lutherans in America* (New York, 1890).

Articles

BERKLEY, HENRY J., "Maryland Physicians at the Period of the Revolutionary War," *Maryland Historical Magazine,* xxiv (1920), 1-7.

CORDELL, EUGENE F., "Charles Frederick Wiesenthal, Medicinae Practicus," *Johns Hopkins Hospital* Bulletin, nos. 112-113 (1900), 170-174.

CUNZ, DIETER (ed.), "Genealogical Notes on Charles Frederick Wiesenthal," *SHGM,* xxviii (1953), 82-85.

ENGELBERT, EDWARD F., "Martini Lutheran Church in Baltimore," *SHGM,* xxvi (1945), 30-32.

EVERS, FRITZ O., "Allgemeine Deutsche Schulzeitung," *SHGM,* xxiv (1939), 38-41.

HENNINGHAUSEN, LOUIS P., "Reminiscences of the Political Life of the German-Americans in Baltimore, 1850-1860," *SHGM,* vii (1893), 51-59; ix (1898), 1-18.

HOFMANN, JULIUS, "Nature and History," *The Reformed Church Review,* xvi (1910), 324-336.

KURTZ, J. DANIEL, "Autobiography," *The Lutheran Observer,* June 1856 and following issues.

MORRIS, JOHN G., "Publications by Lutherans in the United States," *The Evangelical Review,* viii (1856), 273.

REICHMANN, FELIX, "German Printing in Maryland," *SHGM,* xxvii (1950), 9-70.

RUDORF, DR., "Freie Deutsche Gemeinde," *Columbia,* December 1868. (Washington, D. C.)

SCHMUCKER, BEALE M., "The Lutheran Church in York, Pennsylvania," *Lutheran Quarterly,* xviii (1888), 496.

WUST, KLAUS G., "1953—Jahr der Entscheidung für die Zionskirche," *Baltimore Correspondent,* December 16, 1953.

(SHGM—*Society for the History of the Germans in Maryland, Reports)*

INDEX

INDEX

INDEX

Hagerstown, Md., 35, 50, 52.
Hall of Records, Annapolis, Md., 20.
Hamburg (Germany), 115.
Hammer, August, 53.
Hammer, Friedrich, 53.
Hanover, Pa., 29.
Harrison, Mr., 23.
Hartweg, Vitus, 1, 25.
Hartwick, Rev. John C., 13-14.
Heidelbach, J. H., 39.
Helmuth, Rev. Just H. C., 35, 37.
Hildebrandt, A., 69.
Hinrichs, John, 93.
Hoffmann, Daniel, 52.
Hofmann, Adele, 90.
Hofmann, Rev. Julius, 81, 87-103, 137.
Hornell, Rev. Nicholas, 14.
House of Delegates, Maryland, 100.
Hoyer, Rev. John C., 85, 86.
Huber, Henry, 68.
Hymnbooks, 47, 93.

Immigrants, German, 1-3, 26, 27, 36, 81, 85, 97-101, 114.
Immigrants, non-English, 50, 80.
Immigrants, Swiss, 28, 90.
Incorporation, 36, 55.
Indentured Servants, 3, 27.
Independent Church, 71, 86, 102.
Independent Citizens Union, 99.
Infant Mortality, 36.
Innere Mission, 102.
Itinerant Preachers, 3, 11, 13, 34.

Jena (Germany), 34.
Johns Hopkins University, 90.
Julius Hofmann Foundation, 104.

Karthaus, Carl W., 55.
Kirchen-Agende, 45.
Kirchen-Archiv, 1, 17, 19, 63.
Kirchenblatt, 92.
Kirchenmusikverein, 93.

Kirchner, Rev. John C., 11, 14-23, 124.
Kirchtag of Zion, 94.
Knauf, H., 73.
Know-Nothing Movement, 80.
Kohl, Friedrich, 17, 22, 30.
Kraft, Valentine, 3.
Kreuznach (Germany), 64, 65.
Kropp Seminary, 103.
Krug, Rev. J. Andrew, 15.
Kummer, Friedrich, 70.
Kurtz, Rev. Benjamin, 52, 53, 71.
Kurtz, Rev. J. Daniel, 11, 28-58, 61, 64, 67, 69, 71, 72, 89, 126.
Kurtz, Rev. J. Nicolas, 24, 28, 33-35, 45.

Lachey, Rev., 7.
Lancaster, Pa., 21, 24, 34.
Lawson, Alexander, 6-8.
Lebanon, Pa., 35, 41.
Lehrvorträge, 84, 91.
Leipziger Messe, 97.
Less, Rev. Dr., 34.
Levely, George, 30.
Levely, William, 17, 21, 22.
Lexington Street, Baltimore, 44, 91.
Leypold, Friedrich, 52.
Leypold, Johannes, 30.
Liberty Loan Drives, 100.
Liederkranz, 74, 85, 86.
Lindemann, Conrad, 68.
Lindenberger, George, 15, 17, 18, 20-22, 25, 26, 50.
Lindenberger, John, 26.
Lititz, Pa., 36.
Littig, Peter, 30.
Liturgy, 12, 45, 47, 91, 101.
Löble, Wilhelm, 17, 21, 22.
Loerch, Valentine, 6.
Lord Baltimore, 4.
Lord Fairfax, 13.
Lorraine Cemetery, 88.
Low-German Preaching, 105.
Lüdeking, Friedrich, 74.

INDEX

INDEX

INDEX

Members of the Church Council 1954-1955

HANS-LUDWIG WAGNER, Th.D., *Pastor*

HERMANN STEINGASS, *President*

ROBERT E. CARTER, *Vice President*

WILLIAM C. LURSSEN, *Treasurer*

W. KELLER GORSUCH, *Secretary*

ERNST KOEHLER, *Financial Secretary*

PAUL BERT

PAUL R. BUCHWALD

ARNO HABERKORN

ALBERT R. HERDA

GEORGE H. HOKEMEYER

WILLIAM T. HOKEMEYER

CURT A. H. JESCHKE

ALBERT L. JOHN

HERBERT M. METZLER

REINHOLD SCHILLING

CARL F. C. SCHLEUNES

WERNER G. SCHOELER

WALTER VEIGEL

HENRY L. WIENEFELD

WALTER WOERNLE